DATE DUE

OCT 1 3 '95			

TEENAGERS TALK
ABOUT SCHOOL . . .

OTHER BOOKS BY ELAINE LANDAU

Teenagers Talk *about* School...

and Open Their Hearts about Their Closest Concerns

▲

ELAINE LANDAU

Julian Messner

For Jean Dickerson

Published by Julian Messner, a division of
Silver Burdett Press, Inc., Simon & Schuster, Inc.,
Prentice Hall Bldg., Englewood Cliffs, NJ 07632.

JULIAN MESSNER and colophon are trademarks of
Simon & Schuster, Inc.   Design by Claire Counihan
Manufactured in the United States of America.
(Library ed.) 10 9 8 7 6 5 4 3 2 1

(Paper ed.) 10 9 8 7 6 5 4 3 2

Library of Congress Cataloging-in-Publication Data

Landau, Elaine.
    Teenagers talk about school—and open their hearts about their closest
concerns / Elaine Landau.
        p.   cm.
    Summary: Teenagers discuss various aspects of their experiences in school,
including academic and peer pressure, racial and ethnic discrimination,
grades, and drugs.
    1. High school students—United States—Attitudes—Juvenile
literature.   2. High school students—United States—Interviews—Juvenile
literature.   [1. High schools.   2. Schools.   3. Youths' writings.]   I. Title.
LA229.L286   1988
373.18′1′0973—dc19
ISBN 0-671-64568-4 (lib. bdg.)   88–23065
        0-671-68148-6 (paper ed.)   CIP
                                                                                    AC

CONTENTS

FOREWORD

THIS is a book of interviews with junior high and high school students designed to provide a broad-based view of what it's like to attend school in America today. To piece together an inclusive picture of the current school scene, students were selected from both public and private schools, as well as from poor and affluent neighborhoods. Young people attending inner-city schools, exclusive prep schools, and alternative learning programs were sought out as were new young American immigrants. The students who speak in this book come from as far north as Alaska and as far south as Florida.

The interviews revealed that school cannot be viewed solely as a learning place, but must be seen as a social environment as well. The young people interviewed spoke about student-teacher relationships, extracurricular activities, social stress, the clothes codes, and the pressure for high grades and SAT scores. Some told about the drug scene, prom night, and what it's like to feel like an outsider at a place you're forced to be every day.

At times, students found it impossible to separate their feelings about school from other experiences in their lives—such as growing up in a shared custody situation resulting from a bitter divorce or arriving newly in America to face language, cultural, and social barriers at school.

The poignant, funny, reassuring, as well as disturbing aspects of school portrayed here mirror the feelings of today's young teens. Their often moving experiences in America's educational system are crucial to us all. They are especially crucial to those of you who are also in school. School is your world today, and you will be everyone's tomorrow.

TEENAGERS TALK
ABOUT SCHOOL . . .

TRACY

"School is like a tryout for life"

EVERYONE says that you're supposed to be in school to get an education, but what you learn in class is only a fraction of what's actually taking place at school in the halls, the cafeteria, and the yard. To most of the kids I know, looking good is more important than being prepared for class. It's really crucial because if you don't feel you look okay, then you're self-conscious and you won't be able to concentrate for the rest of the day anyway.

It's a well-known fact that appearances are important in

making an impression. My father wears a tie and suit to work every day and he calls it dressing professionally. When my mother's divorced friends go out to singles bars, they wear outfits that would look right on girls my age. Both are trying to create an image or impression of some sort, but when teenagers spend their time or money on things to look better, that's usually considered wasteful.

The way you look often has a lot to do with the way other people act toward you, whether you like it or not. My girlfriend Sandy had a very well developed figure by the time she was twelve. Boys always noticed her right off. They'd whistle or make flirtatious remarks to her out loud. When you walked down the street with Sandy, truck drivers practically fell out of the cabs of their trucks gawking at her. And I can't describe what going with Sandy to the beach was like, when she'd decide to wear her skimpy pink ruffled bikini.

My older sister, on the other hand, is seventeen and has always been as slim and straight as a reed. My mother keeps telling her that she has a model's figure. But it's clear that boys don't respond to her the way they would to a cover girl. I think that she's been on about two dates so far this year.

How you look has a lot to do with how you'll feel about school. I don't think it can be helped. Even the teachers react more to how a student looks than to what's inside. When do they really get to know us, anyway?

If a teacher tells a student to act his age, you can usually safely bet that the kid has a mature appearance and may even look older than he actually is. It's also the tall, impressive-looking boys who usually end up running for student council or who are awarded positions of responsibility. The small, slightly built boys are easily overlooked.

2

At school you learn a lot about social things. And it's not the kind of learning that comes straight from teachers or books. You sort of have to see exactly what it takes to be accepted by others. It's more than just making friends. Learning what's acceptable in different situations is often sort of a trial and error process. You learn from talking to other people, watching people, and sometimes from making some very painful mistakes.

My mother always complains that I spend too much time on the telephone. She thinks that I'm just gossiping with my friends and feels that my time would be better spent studying. She can't seem to understand that my friends and I help each other through some pretty rough situations. She thinks that way because she doesn't believe that anything a teenager does besides homework is important. My Mom tells me to learn in school, but she doesn't realize that I'm actually trying to learn to survive school. Attending school is like a tryout for life. I know that it sounds silly to adults, but at times getting a date, being invited to a certain party, or being chosen to work on the school's newspaper can mean more than getting an A on a test.

Getting through September to June can be like riding on a roller coaster. So much winning and losing is involved. Class rank, passing the road test to get a driver's license, scholarships, college acceptance and social acceptance all may or may not be yours. Sometimes you feel as though you're always holding your breath. There are both exciting and terrifying days.

Much of what's expected socially is new to a lot of us. And it's important to come out looking good. You have to seem mature and sophisticated. You have to be able to keep up a conversation, even if you really have nothing to say to the person you're talking to. You don't want to look stupid. And there's pressure to try a lot of different things—just so you can say that you've done it. If you don't keep up with what the really popular people do, then you're still considered a kid, or worse, really out of it.

That's why a lot of kids take drugs, drink alcohol, or have sex. I hate the taste of liquor. It burns my throat and always gives me a headache. Yet I've forced myself to swallow it and to look like I'm enjoying myself. Beer is even worse. It always tastes like soapy dishwater to me, no matter what brand I try. But I keep up a good pretense. Some kids smoke marijuana to be cool. I think being in possession of an illegal drug that frightens their parents makes them feel important and independent.

All my friends pretend some of the time. In certain situations, you're forced into it. I even know people who've had sex just to get it over with. To have finally done it. This is especially true of the boys. It's like being a virgin was somehow keeping them kids when they desperately wanted to be adults. They have to present themselves as being experienced. It's important to them.

But it doesn't always work. Right now there are four pregnant teenage girls at our school. Within months they'll all be mothers, but they still giggle and exchange notes like the other fifteen- and sixteen-year-olds. It makes you see how young they really are.

These girls walk through the halls at school in their maternity outfits alongside other students who've spent everything they've earned on fall clothes. Whether or not they admit it, everybody wants to be special. They go through the corridors trying to look good, to look sexy, trying to be noticed in the right way. Big hellos are exchanged, and lots of talking and hugging goes on. You can try hard to impress the others, but it's easy to feel self-conscious and

4

awkward when you desperately want to look social and mellow.

Still, that's what so much of school is all about. All the stuff that doesn't necessarily happen in class.

PHILIP

"Kids don't have any rights"

MY school is horrible all year round, but it's worst in the summer when it's hot. The building itself is old—I'm sure that it could be easily classified as an ancient relic. It basically consists of four floors of what looks like crumbling concrete. I think that years ago it might have been a beige color, but now it's taken on a sort of greenish tint.

There are bars on the lower floor windows. The bars are supposed to stop people from breaking in, but when

6

you're sitting in a lower floor classroom or in the downstairs auditorium, it's hard to escape the feeling of being in prison. In fact, the whole building is sort of like a penitentiary. The outside courtyard or playground area has been stripped of all grass and shrubbery, and is now covered with tar and asphalt. The entire yard is enclosed by a wide length of ugly iron fencing. Okay, it's not a barbed wire fence or the kind that instantly electrocutes climbers, but I still think that we practically have a ready made film set for prison courtyard scenes.

The inside of the school is even worse. Our daily lives are regulated by a series of bells that signal us to scurry to our next class. When we studied that poem with the line "Don't ask for whom the bell tolls—it tolls for you," I couldn't help thinking about how our time at school is arranged.

Another warm human touch is our loud speaker system over which our school administration and the school secretary let their wishes be known. It's an old system with enough static to make all the voices broadcast sound sort of raspy and alike.

Often you have to stop what you're doing and strain to hear what was being said over the public address system. Half the time the garble remains garble.

This used to upset the teachers a lot. They'd tell the class to behave and then rush across the hall or next door to piece together the message with another teacher. Naturally, the class usually took this as their cue to begin to riot.

Lately, the system has been somewhat improved. After the voices have left the school's airways, the office sends a girl around to the various classrooms bearing the same message in writing. For some unknown reason, these girls always seem to be sort of pretty, and as they graciously hand the slips of paper to the faculty members, they remind me of the models on the Academy Award shows who bring the envelopes containing the lucky winners' names to the stage.

You can survive my school if you learn to ignore much of what's going on around you, which includes confinement, the petty annoyances, and the humiliation that seem to be part of a public school. My brother who's now in college always says to try to take the best from every situation, and that's what I'm trying to do now.

But during the summer when it's hot and humid and I'm still in a classroom trying to make up a grade for some dumb course, it becomes difficult. It's sweltering in that building, even the walls seem to sweat. To reach all your classes you practically have to run up and down two to three flights of stairs crowded with hordes of sweaty kids. Believe me, we're not being educated in a luxury hotel.

There's an elevator, but it's usually reserved for faculty members and deliveries. There are also several air-conditioned areas in the school. The principal's and vice principal's offices are air-conditioned, and so is the teachers' room. So the same people who earn a salary teaching us that the United States Constitution guarantees equal rights for everyone at least have their own oasis in which to cool off when the thermometer's mercury rises.

My uncle has a civil service job in an unair-conditioned building, but when the temperature and humidity reach a certain level, they close the office and send the staff home. But our school never closes due to the heat. I even read about a zoo in California that air conditions some of its animal shelters because they feel it's inhumane to force the animals to tolerate excessive heat without relief.

But there's no relief for us. We're just supposed to get through it. Two of the three water fountains in the hall don't work at all. There's usually a line at the other water cooler, but the water pressure's so low, you can barely drink from it. Kids don't have any rights in school or anywhere else for that matter. Apparently, zookeepers are more concerned about the lives entrusted to their care.

JONATHAN

"He helped us to lift
all the boundaries"

ONE of the best courses I ever had in school was the English class I took last term. But I didn't feel that way about it from the start. Our teacher, Mr. Baker, was young and new at our school, and he ran the class in a way that was different from anything I'd ever experienced. For example, on the first day of class he refused to tell us either what we'd be covering or what would be required of us. This made everyone feel a little nervous since a lot of those enrolled were honors students and extremely anxious about keeping up their grade point average.

The class was conducted as though it were a college seminar. Our desks were turned around to form a circle; we sat in class facing one another. Baker didn't lecture. Instead, he questioned us in a challenging and provocative manner. Our reactions to the various writers became the essence of the course. Mr. Baker usually added his opinion, but he made it clear that reading and enjoying literature was a subjective process and that there were no right or wrong answers—only personal interpretations. He used to say that each person brings as much to a book as the book brings to him.

You didn't take notes in Mr. Baker's class, which meant that you didn't know how to study for his tests. When we'd ask him what he wanted us to know, he'd say that he was interested only in what we thought about what we had read and our comparisons of the different texts covered.

At first it was hard not to feel uneasy about being unable to study for Mr. Baker's tests in the usual way. A number of kids transferred to different English classes early on in the term. I stayed though, and now I'm really glad that I did. We did so many great things. Our class wasn't always held in the building. Sometimes Mr. Baker would get complimentary tickets to a local playhouse or he'd arrange for us to take part in a poetry festival.

Our final exam was unbelievable. There was only one question on it, and Mr. Baker gave it out to the class several weeks in advance of the test date. You could select any three works we studied and write one to two pages on each.

But it wasn't as easy as it sounds. Our papers could not contain the ideas that we had gone over in class. You had to think of something original. If you included one rehashed idea in your exam booklet, you'd get an automatic C. For two repeated ideas or conclusions, you'd earn a D. If three or more of the ideas we had discussed in class were present on your paper, you'd be taking the course over in summer school.

At first I found Mr. Baker's requirement difficult, in fact, it seemed nearly impossible. After all, some of the smartest kids in the school were in that class, and hadn't they said every brilliant thing imaginable?

Apparently not. After years of being a student, for the first time I had to reach into my own mind to tap my creativity. I came up with a completely original paper, which I even enjoyed thinking about and writing.

Mr. Baker rewarded my efforts by giving me an A on my final. But actually he had done much more for me than that. Mr. Baker had forced us to think of him more as a guide than as an authority. We learned to develop our own thinking. He gave me the courage to accept and value my own interpretations.

Much of what Mr. Baker taught us could be applied to other school subjects as well as to some things in everyday life. It's a critical way of both viewing the world and learning to accept your own feelings. Some of us in his class feel grateful to Mr. Baker for conducting the class as he did. He helped us to lift all the boundaries set on our minds and our spirits—the same kinds of boundaries and pressures that so many of the other teachers use to confine us. Unfortunately, Mr. Baker is no longer at our school. There was some controversy over his refusal to teach the vocabulary lists deemed necessary for the SAT's by the English Department's head.

This year I'm back to studying vocabulary and taking complete sets of notes in my new English class. But what

I'm doing now still hasn't wiped out all the good feelings that I came away with from Mr. Baker's class. I know that he made something wonderful happen to me and to most of the other students who stayed for the term. It was as if he freed a caged bird or untied a chained dog, and you don't easily forget a teacher like that.

J O D Y

"School means so much to me now"

I'M glad I have school because going there provides me with practically the only spot of sanity left in my life. My parents divorced about a year and a half ago. They were deadlocked in a bitter custody fight over me for a number of months. That's really amazing because most of the time I feel that neither of them really wants me living with them. I feel like I'm always in the way.

Anyway, I sort of became the pawn in their power struggle. It was as if both of them really had to win despite the fact that neither seems equipped to care for me on their own. It's okay though, because I take care of myself.

I think there's a saying that goes something like "To the victor belong the spoils." They both won because they ended up having joint custody—I live at my mother's house for part of the week and then at my father's apartment for the remaining days. My weekends are alternated between the two places. This way each of my parents may feel that they've won, but I know that I've lost.

Although my parents live within a mile of each other, being constantly shifted between two places isn't easy. My friends never know where to call me. It's especially hard if you meet a new boy, because boys don't like to call and then have to talk to your parents. It's even worse if the conversation isn't going to result in having you come to the phone.

Besides, neither of my parents takes accurate telephone messages. My mom used to when we all lived together, but now she's too busy tracking her own social life to worry about mine. She doesn't like me to talk on the phone for very long, because she's always worried that a man she's seeing or someone she hopes will call won't be able to get through. She's worse than some of the flightiest girls I know.

If I want to be in a boy's arms he has to have a car or it'll have to happen at a party or in some deserted place. I won't let anyone touch me unless I really like him. But both my parents outdo even the worst kids at school. They constantly bring new people home with them to sleep over. I feel humiliated a lot of the time. It's embarrassing to continually meet people for the first time over the breakfast table when they're still wearing their bathrobes. It's just too clear where they've spent the night.

It's hard to believe that all this is going on when everyone is warning us about new deadly sexually transmitted diseases. We're always being told about AIDS in school. We've seen films, been assigned reports, and there's even been special assemblies on the topic. But I'm afraid that my parents wrongly believe that it'll never happen to them. Don't they care if they're around to see me grow up?

Weekends are the worst. Neither of my parents ever really wants me with them then unless they've just broken up with someone and they're lonely. While they used to fight over who was going to have custody, now the arguments are over who's going to be stuck with me for the weekend. Long weekends and holidays are awful. I remember how things used to be and I do a lot of crying then. Many times I end up staying with my friends and their families.

Since their divorce my mother and father act more like kids than like parents. The woman who cleans my father's apartment found a marijuana roach under one of the couch cushions. She confronted me with the evidence and then proceeded to deliver a long lecture on the perils of drug abuse.

Although I didn't tell her the truth, what she had found hadn't been mine. I wouldn't touch that garbage. I hope to one day play professional women's tennis and I have no intention of polluting my body. But I staged a cover-up for my father, taking all the blame and swearing to her that I'd never do it again. I guess I felt that I had to protect his reputation.

I stopped being a child when my parents split and that's why school means so much to me now. I don't just go there to get an education, although learning is very important to me. At least the grown-ups there still act like adults. I respect several of my teachers a great deal. These people aren't my family, but they've taken more of an interest in me and have more time for me than my parents do.

I know that my parents are going through a rough period, but so am I. I think that school is the only stable part of my existence. Because I lead such a topsy-turvy life, I even enjoy the daily routine of class and the cafeteria that so many kids complain about.

My language arts teacher and my music teacher are my favorite people. I can count on both to be helpful and to provide solid advice. They have a clearer view of things than most of my friends, and right now it's extremely important for me to know that there are adults in my life whom I can depend on.

It's wonderful to be around concerned people who are not continually irritable, angry at you, or overly concerned with themselves. Sometimes I just need to be a kid—to lean on someone who won't let me down. These women allow me to be a teenager, but at the same time they're helping me to grow up. I'm grateful to them both. They've taught me a lot more than English and music theory.

MARLA

"The popular kids represent the American ideal"

YOU can walk into my school and practically tell who's who just by looking around. Actually, the students fall into four different groups. There are the punkers, the burnouts, the popular kids, and the music people.

The punkers are the ones with all the leather, the chains, and the spiked hair in assorted colors. They exclude everyone unless you're part of their group, but a lot of people look down on them anyway. Some kids who don't feel that they're accepted at school become punkers. They may

18

start out by altering their appearance to fit in. Sometimes it doesn't happen all at once; it's more like a gradual change. If they're having social problems and they change into punkers, then they'll usually be accepted in that group. Some punkers are into the antinuclear war thing and other causes like that.

The burnouts are the kids who are into drugs, alcohol, and smoking. They cut class a lot and usually don't do too well in school. There's a smoking lounge at our school, but you need your parents' written permission to use it. During breaks between classes, that's where you'll usually find the burnouts.

In the last couple of years at school there's been a problem with kids using hard drugs. There's also been some trouble with heavy drinking. Kids have actually come to school drunk. Usually the burnouts dress in jeans and wear the black rock-concert T-shirts. Some of the teachers get really uptight about those T-shirts, especially if there's something obscene on them. In that case a teacher or one of the deans may make them change into a gym shirt. Lots of times when these kids are walking in the halls, they'll wear a jacket to cover up what's on their T-shirts. At that point they're trying not to be noticed by the faculty.

I think that if most people at school were really honest about it, they'd admit that they'd like to be in with the popular kids. The popular people are sort of like a big group of friends, although there are definitely smaller cliques within the larger group. They're stylish and dress like miniature preppies.

The popular kids represent the American ideal, but I don't know if their lives are always so ideal. Last year one of the most popular preppie girls at school got pregnant. Nobody at school even thought that she was having sex.

19

She decided to go through with the pregnancy and keep the baby. And all of a sudden she wasn't popular or a preppie anymore.

The music people are the kids at school who are serious about their music. Usually they're in the school band or chorus. Those who sing devote much of their energy to trying out for parts in the school's musicals. They're really good at what they do, and the same kids almost always get the big parts every year.

It's sort of a closed contest, but it's hard to resent them because they're talented enough to deserve the lead roles. The music teachers favor them because they work hard and are good at what they do. Some of those kids play two or more instruments or sing as though they were Broadway bound. These kids are generally liked, although they're out of the popular mainstream. Usually they're good students and do well in most subjects.

Although there are other kids who perhaps fall into special groups of their own, this is just about the way our school shapes up. It's kind of a whole separate world.

DENISE

"To them we're all alike"

IF you're poor, black, and trying to attend high school in a rough neighborhood, chances are that you're going to have to fight for your education. At school you're usually up against more than tough kids or a bunch of macho guys who have to disrupt the few classes they attend in order to show that they're cool and in control. Most of the time you're up against teachers who either seem afraid for their own lives or are just too tired or discouraged to care about their work.

I admit that they have a difficult job. There isn't enough money in the entire world to make me accept a teaching job at my own school if someday I had the credentials to be hired. But even so, the teachers and the administration aren't being fair. Everyone at school has the feeling that to them we're all alike.

Of course, they're more aware of the students who are especially troublesome or even dangerous, but that's not what I'm talking about. At my school you can't help but feel that the faculty doesn't have very high expectations for us because we're black and from poor neighborhoods, and perhaps, ironically, because we're attending their school.

You can forget about all those rags to riches stories that supposedly make up the backgrounds of so many successful Americans. It's clear that our teachers think that we're not going to make it.

Mostly, I think that it's just racism. Unfortunately, that's what being black is too often all about. We're not the middle class token black kids on our way to Harvard. And none of my teachers have personally taken me under their wing to help me to get into a good school or get any type of scholarship or financial aid.

They don't see us that way. Not even those of us who do our homework, study for tests, and go to classes regularly. For girls like us they speak glowingly of careers as key punch operators and bank tellers. If you're an athletic guy, they might think of you as having a slim chance of becoming a professional basketball player.

Yes, this is still happening today—right here in urban America. In this country at a time when Jesse Jackson almost became a candidate for a major political party.

It's happening to some kids at my school in spite of

the fact that they want more for themselves. Being poor is not something that you ever get used to or willingly accept. It only makes you more desperate to change your life—to have a shot at something better.

I'm willing to work to get out of here and become some-body. Martin Luther King had a dream for us. And I have that dream for myself. But it becomes discouraging when the people who are supposed to lead the way out have to be convinced that you're not garbage. That you can rise above it. And most of all that it's their responsibility to help you.

My mother has two jobs. She works in a dry-cleaning store during the day, and two evenings a week and on Sundays she waitresses at a nearby coffee shop. She's the single parent of three daughters, and ever since I can remember, she's always tried to do her best for us. She taught us all how to keep a spotless house, and at times when she's had to take day house-cleaning work on Saturdays to make ends meet, one of us would go along with her to help.

My mother always said that there are two ways to earn a living—either with your brain or with your sweat. She said that it was important to know how to care for your own home, but that if any of her kids ever became a cleaning woman, she would feel as though she'd failed as a mother.

My mother's never failed us in any way. Besides working so many hours a week, she's become active in the PTA. She says that she wants to be there to fight for our right to a decent education.

I know that I have to fight too. I have to do more than just pass the tests at school. I have to get good enough grades to win a scholarship. I need teachers who'll teach, not just act as police officers or cower down before the bullies.

And maybe most of all I need teachers who'll see me as a special person with a chance to make it. They need to see things the same way my mother does and offer the same kind of encouragement to me and the other kids like me at our school. No matter what I do now, to them I'm still a poor black who may at best become a legal secretary. But maybe I'd prefer to be an attorney. And perhaps with enough effort and the right guidance that's what I could become. I know that other young black people have done it, but I don't know of anyone from our school.

Our teachers and guidance counselors still seem to spend most of their energy on the few white kids or even the light-skinned Hispanics at our school. It's a cruel joke. A lot of those kids are on drugs and don't seem to care about anything at all. They're only about one step away from dropping out of school altogether. Yet these kids are often seen as the ones who could possibly turn their lives around. Why do they think of them that way? The only thing they seem to have going for them is the color of their complexion in a racist society. But unfortunately, maybe that's enough.

I'm dark and I've got a lot going for me. So do my sisters, and there are others like us. But our teachers seem content to leave us alone. I think it's easier for them that way.

I don't know where our faculty was during the '60s civil rights movement. Did they sleep through it or have they just turned off to all of us because of the tough kids they're forced to deal with? Even now in the '80s, to them white or light is beautiful, and sometimes I feel as though I've got to work doubly hard to prove them wrong. It may seem like a peculiar position for a student to be in, but that's the way it is.

24

STEVEN

"Mediocre will do"

IF a Martian landed on Earth, and I had to advise him on how to get through an American junior high or high school, I think I'd quote the biblical saying "The meek shall inherit the earth." None of this Darth Vader or laser beam fancy stuff. Even someone from another planet could graduate if he just learned to show up on time, shut his mouth, and not make waves.

Most teachers like to have their sense of power and being in charge underscored. You have to stick to their rules even if they are obviously unfair. The teachers are the drill sergeants and we're the new recruits. You don't have to be smart to get a diploma. Mediocre will do, if you don't cause any trouble. The last thing a harried teacher wants is another irritation or a bothersome student. If you're not a discipline problem and you do the homework most of the time, you'll make it. Teachers like to feel that what they're doing is important. We're supposed to be the sponges—they're the water.

Our teachers may say that they long for bright, stimulating students, but when they're faced with classes of over thirty of us for five periods a day, they're grateful for the cheerful, polite, and orderly student, even if that person is intellectually dead. Killed by having successfully completed junior high, that person may be going through high school as a zombie.

Our vice principal is really authoritarian. If he were a storybook character he'd be the troll waiting under the bridge to devour a small child or perhaps a billy goat. He doesn't see us as young people with feelings. To him, kids are a sort of subspecies of the human race.

In fact, our whole school administration has no respect for the students' privacy or dignity. Once the vice principal had the janitor forcibly open a kid's locker because he suspected that the boy had a hidden stash of drugs there. Even though they rummaged through all the kid's personal stuff, they didn't find what they were looking for. The vice principal's suspicions had been off target, but nobody even apologized to the boy.

They hadn't needed a search warrant to do what they did. Yet, if the police did the same thing to them, they'd probably sue the cops in court for harassment or invasion of privacy or something like that.

Maybe we'd be better off if Martians did come to Earth and somehow gained control of our schools. At least there'd be new lesson plans. And maybe they'd bring a fresh approach to the classroom. Perhaps to them kids would just appear to be wrinkle-free young people, and not a subspecies of the human race.

CHRISTINE

"I had been wanting to go to the prom for such a long time"

I really wanted to go to my junior prom. I'd been going with my boyfriend Danny for eight months and all along I'd just assumed that we'd be there together. All my friends planned to go, and for the past few weeks that seemed to be the only thing anybody talked about.

The problem was that the prom was dreadfully expensive. And I think that I must have been the poorest kid attending an exclusive private school. My parents had scrimped and done without things themselves in order to send me there. I'm their only child—as a matter of fact, I'm adopted—

and it was important for them to feel that they were giving me the best education that money could buy. They really didn't have the money.

In any case, they paid the tuition and I worked for a few hours every day after school and on weekends to help to pay for my clothes and the other things I needed. From four to six I worked putting away books at the public library. That's not as bad as it sounds, because I always got first crack at all the books we needed for school assignments. Because I put the books and magazines away, I knew exactly where everything was.

After I finished at the library, I baby-sat from six to eight in the evening for a really nice lady who lives two doors away from us. She has three of the most wonderful little boys. I used to think of them as my little brothers. I'd help her fix dinner, eat with the boys, and then help them to get ready for bed. They're a nice family and they always gave me a little extra money for the time I spent at their home.

My junior prom cost $250. It was being held at a fancy nightclub in the city. My mother thought that the whole thing was bizarre. She said that her junior prom took place in the high school gym. A group of girls on the prom committee had decorated the entire area with flowers made out of toilet paper. My mother said that the decorative highlight was the waterfall they fashioned from cut up strips of Saran Wrap.

But although she felt that my prom was extravagant, my mother still supported my going because she knew how badly I wanted to go. And besides, she had often said that she was proud of me for having saved up nearly all the money for it by holding down two jobs—without letting my grade point average fall.

Still, as prom time drew closer, it didn't look good—

$250 was just the price of admission. I'd need a dress, shoes and bag, and I'd have to have my hair done. I'd looked at evening dresses, and all the pretty ones were outrageously high. My mother had taken sewing lessons, but even she admitted that her skills were limited and that she'd never be able to put together anything as elaborate as a gown.

But after shopping around for a while, we did find something nice that was fairly affordable. And my cousin, who wore the same shoe size as me, offered me this gorgeous pair of silver heels with a matching purse that she had worn only once, to her boyfriend's sister's wedding.

However, my prom problems still weren't over. There was yet another tremendous obstacle to overcome—transportation. How were Danny and I going to get there? Everybody we were friends with were renting limousines for the evening. Their families could obviously afford it. But the cost was sky high, and Danny, who went to a Catholic boy's school across town, came from a family with even less money than mine. Danny didn't have his license yet, and besides, both our families had old compact cars. There was even a big dent in the side of our car, which my parents had never bothered to have fixed.

I decided that if I couldn't ride to the prom in some sort of style, I'd rather not go at all. It wouldn't be any fun if you were embarrassed all evening.

And for a while it seemed as though that was the way it was going to turn out. My parents would have had to help me to raise the $250 admission cost, and that didn't include any of the other essentials. I felt terrible about asking them for a dime for the prom. My father, a bus driver, had been in a serious accident close to a year ago, and he hadn't been back to work since that time. Although he received disability payments at home, the amount of money coming in was considerably less than his salary had been. My mother worked as a secretary. She didn't make much money, and lately there had hardly been any overtime available at her office.

Sometimes I felt as if I should have been giving the money I made to my parents instead of saving it for the prom, but both my parents insisted that I go. They knew how much it meant to me, and I could see how much I meant to them.

As it happened, the neighbor for whom I baby-sat proved to be my fairy godmother. She said that no other sitter had ever made her boys as happy as I had. She told me that she wanted me to go to the "ball." I was beginning to feel like Cinderella.

She and her husband owned a beautiful, brand new, brown Mercedes, and her husband had offered to drive Danny and me to the prom in it. It wouldn't be the same as going in a limo, but it was certainly acceptable, and I had been wanting to go to the prom for such a long time.

Then, on the night of the prom, the most wonderful thing happened. At the exact moment that Danny and I were to be picked up, a gorgeous, silver stretch limousine pulled into our driveway. The chauffeur rang our doorbell and explained that the limo as well as his services as our driver were ours for the evening courtesy of the people I had baby-sat for.

At first I couldn't believe it. I felt better than Cinderella; now I think I know how Queen Elizabeth must feel on her outings. There were tears in my mother's eyes as she listened to the driver, but I couldn't stop smiling . . . giggling, in fact. I was thrilled.

Danny and I went to the prom the way I'd always dreamed

of going. Afterward, the driver took us to several night spots. It was fantastic. I think it was the best night of my life.

My parents took pictures of Danny and me at the house before we left, and there were also other photos from the prom itself. But my favorite shot—the one I take out to look at over and over again—is the picture my mother took of us standing alongside the long silver limousine.

ALLAN

"She handed the car keys over to him"

GETTING my driver's license had to be the highlight of my senior year. My birthday wasn't until late March, so I was among the last of my friends to take the road test. But I'd completed driver's ed at school and knew how to drive months before.

If you asked the guys at school whether they were more excited about graduating from high school or getting their driver's license, I think that most of those who answered honestly would vote in favor of the license. Getting a license sort of officially makes you an adult. You're not dependent on your parents to cart you around anymore.

It's instant manhood. Girls admire the guys with cars. If a really good-looking girl isn't sure whether or not she wants to go out with a particular guy, driving the right car might just make the difference.

Driver's ed was a snap for me. I had already learned a lot from my dad and older brother and had spent time on the road with them. I'd also gone around with some of my friends who already had their licenses. By the time I had signed up for driver's ed I was already a pretty fair driver, but it was important to take the course anyway. If you completed the driver's ed program at school, you paid less for insurance. You also learned what you needed to know in order to get through the road test.

When it was time for me to take the road test, I passed it on my first try. That's really unusual for someone my age. The inspectors are extremely strict, and everyone thinks that they purposely fail teenage boys regardless of the individual's driving skill.

They're definitely prejudiced against us. But no one seems to care because they think that the high teen accident rate justifies that kind of discrimination. Most kids have to take the road test two or three times. I guess that that's their way of keeping us off the road for a while longer.

However, our high school has been working on a program with the county to help promote safe driving habits among young people. We've seen several films and heard different lectures on the importance of wearing seat belts and the hazards of drunk driving.

You hear that stuff, but you never think that it applies to you. If you know that you're a skilled driver, you tend to feel that you can pull off any stunt on the road and still avoid having an accident. If you think that you're sharper, more alert, and have better reflexes than the next guy, you don't always take the warning seriously.

Most of my friends and I felt that driving was a lot like getting good at video games. It takes coordination to begin with, and then it becomes little more than a matter of fine-tuning your ability.

Anyway, that's how we all felt until the night of Brittany's party. It was a rainy Friday night, and Brittany, a junior at school, was giving a Halloween party mainly because her parents were away somewhere for the weekend. Brittany's father was a sports car enthusiast and though he was the only one in the family who drove, Brittany's family still owned two cars.

One of the two was this really great, shiny, red Corvette. My friend Bert begged Brittany to let him take it for a spin. Brittany explained that her father had forbidden her to even open the garage door during his absence. Still, Brittany had had a relentless crush on Bert for the past two years in spite of the fact that he had never asked her out. Although Brittany tried to be firm at first, she seemed to weaken as Bert continued to plead with her. And after about twenty minutes of phony compliments and promises, she handed the car keys over to him.

I wanted to try out the car, but I felt a little unsure about going for a ride with Bert just then. He had had about half a dozen beers and he seemed pretty high. But Bert assured me that the drinking hadn't affected him at all. He said that he was as sharp as ever.

I knew that Bert was a really good driver, so I decided to come though it had been raining steadily all night and I knew that by now the roads must be pretty slick. I never imagined that within the hour I'd regret my decision to go more than anything I'd ever done.

Bert had quick reflexes. But he liked to take chances

and he wasn't known for his patience. Bert usually drove above the speed limit and often tailgated slower cars until he could pass them. Still, Bert had never hit anything. He always said that he could stop in an instant. I learned only later that making an instant stop while exceeding sixty miles an hour was impossible.

That Friday night on the road Bert was angrily cursing out a small Volkswagen in front of us that he felt was going too slowly. I told him to take it easy. All the cars but ours had slowed down due to the heavy rains that evening. We were in the right lane. Bert could have switched lanes easily enough, but instead he seemed determined to bully the Volkswagen into speeding up.

We were only inches from the other car's rear when Bert must have realized that at the speed we were going in the rain, it was becoming really dangerous. But as Bert continued to assure me that he was still in control and knew just what he was doing, I realized that he had no idea of how the beer had affected his judgment.

It happened less than an instant later. Another car entered the roadway, cutting off the Volkswagen in front of us. The Volkswagen slowed down to avoid a collision with the on-coming vehicle. But Bert wasn't able to stop in time.

We plowed into the Volkswagen from the rear with such force that the small car spun across the middle and left lanes of the highway. It finally came to a stop, crashing into the highway divider that separated us from the traffic going in the opposite direction.

The car had landed on its side. For the next few seconds, Bert and I just gazed at the car across the highway. It was hard to move. I couldn't believe what had happened. Bert, who had been the big macho man only moments before, began to shake and hiccup. His cheeks were tear stained.

The traffic on our side of the highway had come to a

complete stop. A number of people had left their cars to help, and by the time we reached the Volkswagen, two men had pulled a young woman driver from the car.

They placed her on the ground and covered her with a blanket. One of the men had turned the girl's head in order to give her artificial respiration. At that point all you could see of her was a limp body with a long mane of tangled sandy blond hair that was matted with blood. As the man moved away we saw the girl's face for the first time.

I ran to the side of the road. I knew that I was about to throw up and I couldn't stop myself. The girl driving the Volkswagen couldn't have been more than seventeen years old. She was just a kid like us.

The young girl whose car we hit will never be able to walk again without assistance. When we visited her in the hospital for the last time, she was learning to use a walker. The accident affected her in other ways as well; her speech and vision will be permanently distorted.

The girl's mother told us that her daughter had wanted to be a dancer. I know that she'll never be anything like that now. It was like a beautiful china doll had been smashed and broken. But what makes it so awful is that the girl is a real human being.

It's been like a bad dream. Bert lost his license and he may also be facing criminal charges. Bert's being blamed, but I feel as though it's partly my fault as well. I knew that Bert was high. I keep thinking that maybe if I'd been a real friend, I'd have stopped Bert instead of just going along with what he wanted to do.

But it's too late now for that kind of thinking. I can't just jump into a time machine and go back to change what happened that night. I know that I can never make it up to the girl who was hurt.

Nothing I can do means very much now. She's lost so

much. And everyone who knew her has lost a lot as well. But you can't take away someone's pain or give them back the life they had. And as hard as it is to deal with, I'm going to have to face the fact that I'm partly responsible for what happened on that rainy night.

Author's note: During her recovery period, the young female victim made two attempts to take her own life. Unfortunately, she succeeded on the third try. The girl died the same week that her senior class graduated. Neither Allan nor Bert have been available for comment.

BRAD

"They cursed and ridiculed Stu"

THIS fall our school sponsored an open house
for parents, local businessmen, and other interested members of the community. The halls were decked with the
best work of our art classes, demonstrations of the various
applications of our new computers ran nonstop in our computer lab, and the school orchestra's music filtered up from
the auditorium to fill the corridors and classroom areas.

A number of students had been selected by the faculty
to serve as hosts and hostesses that evening. Supposedly,

we had been picked on the basis of our grade average, good character, and active participation in extracurricular activities. Our principal had described us as the best our school had to offer.

Each host or hostess was to take several small groups of visitors on guided tours of the school's building. After telling the guests a bit about our school lives and our ambitions, we were to point out the high points and interesting aspects of the school facility and answer any questions we were asked.

My own biographical speech went something like this—"Hi, I'm Brad Furman. I'm vice president of the junior class, president of the debating club, I maintain a 92 average and am currently on the basketball and track teams." On one of the tours, before I could go any further, a middle-aged woman in my group raised her hand to ask a question. When I responded, she said, "Brad, you seem like an all-American dream. I think we need more young men like yourself. Do you have a girlfriend? Because if you don't, I have a niece that you'd be absolutely perfect for." Everyone chuckled in agreement, and the tour proceeded pleasantly enough.

That night as I lay in my bed, I couldn't sleep. I was thinking about what that woman had said. It was clear that I had done it again. I'd managed to come across as the typical teenage male headed straight up the ladder to success.

No one knew the truth. No one even suspected. I had become everything I was supposed to be. Our pastor had even made a habit of introducing me as "A bright young man who has it all." It certainly looked as though I did. I had looks, good grades, athletic prowess, and a way with words.

BRAD

I didn't have a girlfriend yet, but everyone thought that was because I was kind of shy and much too busy. But I knew that wasn't the truth. The real reason that there wasn't a girl in my life was locked down deep inside of me where I had kept it hidden for years. I tried not to feel it. I tried not to think about it, but as time passed it was becoming increasingly difficult for me. I think I'm gay.

I can't handle it. I've thought too much about what the consequences would be for me if I am gay. I know what being gay at our school would be like. Instant ostracism. All that I had accomplished previously would vanish. I'd be known only as the gay guy, or much worse than that.

As far as I know, there aren't any other gay people at school now. It had recently become known though that Stu, the school's football captain who graduated three years ago, turned out to be gay. He came out last year while he was away at college.

When the news broke, the guys on the football team wanted to kill him. They cursed and ridiculed Stu, and inked out his face in the school's team photograph. Everyone said that Stu had disgraced the school, and there had even been some talk about ganging up on him to give him the beating of his life if he dared to come home over Christmas vacation. The guys seemed to think that Stu had it coming to him for what he had done to them.

All the talk made me want to crawl out of my skin. Just days before Stu's sexual preference had become known, he'd been considered a school hero. Now he was trash to be smashed down into the ground.

The most unfair part was that Stu had done nothing to any of them. Perhaps he had just found the courage to be who he actually was. If I'd dreaded facing my feelings before, seeing what happened to Stu certainly hadn't helped any.

I'm not certain that I'm gay. Although I've never been with another male sexually, at times I've felt drawn to certain men. I can't help it. Sometimes I've had sexual dreams about other boys, and last year I admired our coach in a way that most people at my school wouldn't consider normal.

I know that I feel much more deeply for my friends than they do for me or for any other guy for that matter. They've all had girlfriends by now, and in that sense I've begun to grow apart from them.

The girls at our school, or anywhere else, aren't exciting to me in the same way that they are to other boys. There were two girls I liked, but only as friends. One of them was Christy, an unusually witty person whom I had enjoyed working with both on the school newspaper and the student council. Christy and I began spending a good deal of time with one another because we were on so many of the same committees.

I enjoyed her company and friendship, but unfortunately Christy viewed me as a potential boyfriend. When I didn't respond to her hints to take her out, she resolved the situation by inviting me to a school girl-ask-boy dance.

I really didn't want to go. I liked Christy, but wasn't interested in her romantically, and didn't want to mislead her. I told her that I had something else to do that weekend, but she continued to try to convince me. Thinking that I was just shy, Christy hardly let a day go by without bringing up the subject.

Meanwhile, my male friends had begun to talk about the dance. Most of them had been asked, and a few were even beginning to brag about how they thought they'd "get lucky" afterward when they went to park at Passion Puddle. Word had gotten around that Christy had asked me, and everybody had begun to tease me about going.

While we were changing out of our gym clothes in the boys' locker room, my best friend Larry had jokingly said in a lispy voice, "Brad, if you don't start going out with girls soon, we're going to think that you're just another Stu." And as I watched him comically wiggle around the locker room while dangling a limp wrist, I knew that I was going to have to accept Christy's invitation.

I was aware that I was using Christy as part of my cover-up, and I didn't like myself for it. Christy Halpern had never been anything but nice to me. Still, I felt pressured to go to the dance, and Christy really wanted me to accept.

I went to the dance and had a good time in spite of all my anxieties about it. All my friends were there, and as usual, Christy was fun to be with. After the dance, I took Christy out for something to eat and then directly home.

I never mentioned Passion Puddle or anyplace like that. I had held Christy's hand, kissed her good night, and felt that I had done my duty for the evening. Nothing more.

That was the way I always handled the few dates I went on. The girls usually attributed my lack of sexual aggressiveness to either my being shy or my having a great deal of respect for them. So far my behavior had passed as acceptable, because the girls I had gone out with were only evaluating a first date. I made sure that there was never a second time. In that way I limited the pressure to go further with them than I wanted to.

But with Christy things turned out differently. We had already become good friends before the dance, and my not asking her out in return cost me her friendship. She never said anything about it; Christy only wrote me a lengthy note saying that she was tired of pursuing me and of being rejected and made a fool of. She even quit the school newspaper so that she wouldn't have to see me as often. I never answered her note or tried to explain. How could I ever tell her what was going on inside of me? I couldn't afford to take a chance on exposing what I felt. I wasn't even sure about what was happening to me anyway. There was no room for anyone who was different at my school. It took all my energy just to go on pretending to be the all-American high school boy.

MARTY

"It wasn't necessary to kill all those frogs"

WE had to dissect frogs in my biology class. Their discolored bodies were doled out to us from prepackaged jars of formaldehyde. When our teacher unscrewed the jar lids the smell was atrocious. It was potent enough to sting your eyes if you came too close.

After we cut the frogs' torsos and separated their tissues, we had to pin their bodies open on pieces of cardboard. Then we drew arrows on the boards in pen to label the various body parts and organs.

Some kids were completely confused and really fouled up the labeling. Some made a joke of the exercise, drawing cartoonlike captions alongside of the dead frogs' brains. Others even wrote catchy phrases near the reproductive organs.

Two girls, working jointly on a frog, brought in different colored magic markers with which to complete the labeling process. Another girl, seemingly determined not to be outdone by their efforts, used thinly sliced strips of brightly colored ribbons to replace the ink drawn arrows.

Our teacher strung the cardboard configurations around the room on what looked like a thin clothesline. The frog bodies still reeked of formaldehyde. We had to keep the windows open most of the time, and the breeze caused the frog corpse boards to sway with the wind as though they were doing a dance.

I don't see the point of having high school students dissect frogs. At school assemblies, we've had to endure countless speeches on the importance of being moral and fair-minded, yet I think that the broad-based destruction of animal life across America for high school biology courses is indecent.

Perhaps some experimentation must be done on animals by doctors and biomedical researchers in the interests of science. Still, lately I've done a lot of reading on that subject, and I'm not even sure how necessary much of that is. Besides, often the animals are treated with unnecessary cruelty by the experimenters.

But I firmly believe that no animal should have to die for the benefit of a high school student's knowledge. We're not advancing science. Most of the kids spent the period giggling or choking or coughing from the formaldehyde fumes.

All we did was look at the frogs' vital organs and label

them. The same results could have been achieved from studying a chart, a diagram in a book, a computer program, or even a plastic model.

It's ironic because our biology teacher is a devout Catholic who is adamently opposed to abortion. But are the lives of small animals so unimportant to him that he can pay no mind to their useless deaths?

Animals feel pain. They run from their natural predators as well as fight for their lives when cornered and challenged. But they're no match for humans. It wasn't necessary to kill all those frogs for our biology class. In fact, when a number of the female frogs were cut open, they were found to be pregnant. Their fertilized eggs had to be scooped out and tossed into the trash basket before the students working on them could proceed with the labeling.

At times some of the students from the various biology classes have spoken out against what's being done. But their complaints are never dealt with seriously. This year when one boy raised the issue, his biology teacher made light of his comments, and suggested that perhaps he was just too squeamish to complete the dissection. The teacher's reaction served as a cue to the boy's classmates to chime in, and before long the questioning student was busily cutting away at his frog. They had turned the dissection into a challenge to his masculinity.

As you get older it's hard not to be aware of the many contradictions we come across in school as well as in other areas of our lives. "Thou shalt not kill" is a sacred religious commandment as well as an accepted moral standard. But capital punishment has been reintroduced in a number of states. And it's supposed to be acceptable to kill in times of war or in self-defense.

Science is not advanced when animals are mutilated by

a bunch of joking kids who may not even learn anything from their actions. Still, this is exactly what's happening at a high school that claims to try to instill a sense of decency and humanity in its students in the hope of making them better citizens. But how can we be respectable citizens if we have to deny our consciences or ignore our respect for all forms of life in order to pass biology?

PAUL

"Things at home took a turn for the worse"

I don't think it's fair the way some kids get to sail through life, while others of us have to work for everything we get. Parents are supposed to take care of their kids while we're growing up leading carefree lives. But too often it's the other way around.

My parents split when I was little, and my father has always been unreliable about making child support payments. So when my brother and I were young we had to do without a lot of the things that other kids had. I never had the kind of clothes I really wanted. Sometimes I felt too ashamed to go to school. I remember that I used to lie to my mother and say that I was too sick to go to school so I wouldn't have to face the other kids.

A lot of the guys rode their bikes to school. Some of them had pretty sleek models too. I always wanted a new bike with all the extras, but it was out of the question. My mother dug up this old, horrible thing that her cousin must have ridden twenty years ago. I was supposed to act grateful for it. I was afraid to tell my mother how I really felt about the bike because she was angry so much of the time when we were growing up. But I still hated that thing. And I refused to ever ride it to school. My mom just called me a spoiled, selfish kid and let it go at that.

As I got older things got a little better. Not because my father was sending us any more money, but because I was finally able to change some things about my life. I got a job in a fast food place. I worked evenings and weekends. The other kids I worked with were all right. But the job wasn't all that great because we were expected to do a lot of hard physical work. Usually I remained on my feet for just about the whole time I worked, and we were only allowed a ten-minute break.

I worked long hours, but I never seemed to earn enough money. I had to give my mother most of my paycheck because she really needed bread to keep our household going. I also bought my little brother a few things because I remember how awful it was to want what other kids have but not be old enough to earn what you needed to buy it. The rest I kept for myself, and I enjoyed having the spending money.

More than anything else in the world I wanted my own car. But like the bike we had never been able to afford, the car became another financial impossibility. Some of the kids at school came from families in which there were two or three cars. But for us, even a used car would have been an unthinkable luxury.

Meanwhile, things weren't going too well for me at school. I hardly had any time to study or do homework. My teachers complained that I lacked motivation. I guess I have to admit that to some degree they were right.

I felt tired and discouraged a lot of the time. When I wasn't in class or working, I didn't feel like hitting the books. I wanted to listen to music, watch some videos, and spend time with my girlfriend Lisa.

Lisa felt the same way I did about school. To her it was a waste of time that she was pushing herself through to please her parents. We were always being told how valuable an education was, but there was no way that either someone like Lisa or myself could have gone on to college. It would be impossible for either of us to get a scholarship, our grades were too low to ever begin to compete with the other applicants. The grinders—the kids who had dedicated their lives to getting good grades and high scores on advanced placement tests—had the scholarship money sewn up.

Then, at the end of my junior year, any glimmer of hope I might have ever had about going to college was stomped out for good. Things at home took a turn for the worse. The company my mother had been working for went out of business, and she lost her job. After three months of steady job-hunting she had been willing to take a pay cut, however, she still hadn't found anything.

That meant that I had to go to work full time at the fast food place to help out. Since my mother firmly insisted that I not drop out of school, I had to work the night shift. I'd get home at about five o'clock in the morning, and then have to get up at seven to be at school on time. As you can imagine, I was usually late. Once after I fell asleep in English class, my teacher sent me to the vice principal's office.

After a stern lecture from the vice principal, I was shuttled off to the guidance counselor's cubicle for what I guess they thought of as "guidance." That man was the worst. He really didn't know me; all he seemed to go by were my school records.

Anyway, after telling me to take a seat in his office, he said, "Son, I've been looking at your test scores and your grades, and it's clear to me that you aren't working at your full academic potential. You know that a kid's job is to go to school and do well, so why don't you just buckle down and go to work."

I didn't know how to answer him. It was clear that he hadn't even looked into my personal background. And I don't think he really cared either. It seemed as if he just enjoyed hearing himself deliver a sermonlike pep talk. Well, if going to school was my "real" job, then what was I doing for thirty-five hours every week at the fast food place. I couldn't believe that I had been sent to this man for guidance or help or whatever they wanted to call it. I think that someone needs to tell him about what life is really like for a lot of kids. He may have been looking right at me, but he never saw me.

KEVIN

"Their spirits have been pushed aside"

SCHOOL is so boring that I wouldn't go if I didn't have to. I count off the days in the week, then I count off the class periods during the day, sometimes I even count the minutes in each period. Fifty-minute units of boredom. That's what classes are like at my school.

In some ways everybody's a phony at school. The kids pretend to pay attention in order to get a good grade or a college recommendation letter. But the teachers get us back. They stand in front of the class and pretend to teach.

Some of my teachers stick strictly with their lesson plans. They're so regimented that you'd think they were trained in the army. They get really nervous and thrown off if the class discussion interrupts what they had intended to cover that day.

But sometimes those discussions are the best part of the class. Yet that doesn't count. To many teachers any expression of our thoughts, feelings, and reactions means little more than wasted class minutes.

Some of those lesson plans seem to be really outdated. I wonder if they used the same ones on our parents. Most of the teachers just spout information. They have to cover the curriculum, and they don't care if they're boring us to tears.

The kids who show any originality or creative thinking are usually typed as not mastering the material. The praise goes to the conformers who complete the prescribed assignments and tests by filling in the answer blanks correctly. These are the same kids who sit attentively and obediently through class and are complimented for being able to follow directions. They remind me of a group of well-trained dogs. Their spirits have been pushed aside, as they anxiously wait for a pat on the head from their trainer.

The best experience I've had in three years of high school took place outside the classroom in an experimental learning program. And there are others who feel the same way about the program as I do. We were given the opportunity to earn credits for doing community service work. Some of us worked in day care centers and nursing homes. Others were assigned special placements with mentally retarded children as well as in other areas.

I worked at a nonprofit animal shelter. It was great, because in addition to caring for lost and wounded animals,

I found that I was really able to help the staff there. Although I was a teenager, my duties weren't limited to just cleaning out the cages. While I still had time to comfort the animals, I was also given a wide range of special tasks and responsibilities. I was treated as a needed and valued staff member, not just as a kid, and I lived up to the expectations of my supervisors.

Much of my time was spent with the volunteer publicity director. Her work was crucial since the shelter needed money badly and she conducted the fund-raising campaigns. I helped with several direct-mail campaigns, and she even taught me to write simple press releases.

I had always had a flair for writing, but now my writing skills were really sharpened. I learned more about sentence structure and style from that placement than from any English class I had ever been in. It really made me wonder how much more we could get out of school if what we learned were presented to us differently. What would happen if kids were taken as seriously as teachers?

I don't think my school or my teachers will ever change. Unfortunately, most kids will never have my good experience because the community service program at our school has been cut from the curriculum. Now things are back to normal in our classrooms—that means back to being boring most of the time.

KAREN

"When my parents split"

MY parents are divorced, and my stepmother really ruined my existence for a while. First, she invaded my home, and then she tried desperately to be a part of my life at school. My dad adores her all the more for taking such an interest in me, but I often wish she'd go away.

When my parents split, I was supposed to live with my mom and see my dad on weekends. Most of the kids at school from divorced homes live with their mothers. But in my case, it was a disaster. Even with the money from

56

my father, there still never seemed to be enough. While she used to have a part-time job, now my mother worked full-time. She was also taking courses at night to be eligible for a promotion. I hardly ever saw her, and even when I did she was a bundle of nerves. She felt so anxious and guilty over not having enough time to spend with me that what little time we did share was spent fighting.

On the other hand, weekends with my dad were just perfect. We always spent most of the time together. We'd go out for hamburgers or pizza for lunch, and then we'd usually make dinner together. I was Daddy's girl and I loved every minute of it.

Of course, all that was B.C.—before my stepmother, Carla, arrived. Carla is the opposite of my mother. She's nothing like me either. She doesn't have our green eyes, freckles, or red frizzy hair. Carla is slim, dark, and exotic-looking. She has long, shiny, black hair, and she's thinner than me. Although she's always tried to be nice to me, I've hated Carla from the first day we met.

When my dad married Carla, life with Mom really took a turn for the worse. My mother resented Carla even more than I did. She complained that now that Dad had a new wife, there'd be less time and money for me. She said that my father's remarriage would leave her even more burdened than before.

As my mother became increasingly agitated, she and my father seemed to have arguments every time he picked me up or phoned the house. Once she threw a lamp at him, screaming, "If you think living with a teenager is so easy, you just try raising her." And that's exactly what my father did.

And it would have been wonderful too, if living with Dad hadn't meant living with his lovely new wife as well.

Carla tried to be decent, but her presence in the apartment meant that I was no longer the lady of the house at my dad's. Carla was younger than my mother, with no children of her own. My dad had made it clear before they married that he didn't want any more children. So all of Carla's pent up maternal instincts were let loose on you-know-who.

She said that she loved having a daughter. But I already had a mother. Carla wasn't going to take no for an answer. I had become my stepmother's new career.

I had to start a new school in the middle of the term—that would have been bad enough without having Carla there to help me adjust. While my father was at work, Carla enrolled me in school herself. She introduced herself to the school secretary and the vice principal as my mother, but I referred to her only as my father's wife. Fortunately, after a few glaring glances from me, she lessened her title to that of stepmother.

You can't imagine what it was like having her there. It was as though I were five years old and she were bringing me to my first day at kindergarten. Carla was all smiles and she insisted on meeting everyone present. It took the academic guidance counselor close to ten minutes to convince her that it wasn't necessary for her to stay to help me plan my class schedule, and that she was free to leave.

Carla went home that day, but she didn't stay there for long. She took part in every school activity open to parents. In less than three months she was running for office in the PTA, working as a volunteer parent-coordinator in our school's anti-drug program, and playing accompanist piano for our school's production of *Romeo and Juliet.*

Dad couldn't understand my initial negative reaction to Carla's interest in me. But I couldn't be sure whether she actually cared for me or if she just wasn't fascinated with the novelty of gaining an instant daughter.

Sometimes I thought that her interest in me stemmed from a need to please my dad and prove to him that she had accepted me. And to please him as well, I did my best to be nice to Carla. I think that I was ashamed of my jealousy, but I couldn't help what I felt.

And in all fairness, there were some benefits to Carla's playing mother and having her so visible at school. There were a few instances in which I enjoyed pretending that I belonged to her. Especially when I saw how the other kids reacted to her. Carla was much younger than the other parents, and everybody was always saying how gorgeous she was.

I had instantly become the daughter of a glamour queen in a new school where no one knew my real mother, and sometimes it didn't feel half bad. Although I didn't look like Carla, people still tended to think that we were related, and the head of our dance department, whom I had fallen madly in love with the first week of school, had referred to us as "the pretty pair."

Instantly, the child my mother hadn't had time for turned into a rare and precious jewel that was being ruthlessly stolen from her by Dad's new wife. My mother hounded Dad about it constantly. She'd call us several times a week protesting that she was being systematically shut out of my life.

My mother's retaliation was swift. She decided to become more involved in my life. Naturally, the area she claimed for herself was my school, Carla's chosen province. Why couldn't she have opted for buying me clothes? I guess that she needed to cancel out my stepmother more directly.

I was the monkey in the middle. You can't imagine what

it's like to have two women attend a PTA meeting and both claim to be your mother. My father didn't like what my mother was doing, but he said that he was unable to stop her. It was horrible and humiliating, and as they both took part in bake sales and attended band concerts, I was always torn as to who to be with.

Everyone kept asking me which was my biological mother, whom did I like best, and did Carla steal my father away from my mother? I became an overnight curiosity. I felt as though I had to answer a billion questions and explain my parents' divorce over and over.

I began to hate school. And I decided that if the adults in my life were so intent on going to my school, then they could have it all to themselves. For the first time, I began cutting classes on a regular basis.

Eventually, things worked out because of my favorite guidance counselor, Ms. Emory. Ms. Emory had taken a liking to me immediately, and had befriended me since I'd started at the new school. She had sensed what was happening, and we spoke about it for almost an hour in her office. I felt as though, for the first time in a long while, a concerned adult was really interested in my feelings and in what I had to say. Ms. Emory saw to it that no action was taken against me for cutting class. She said that I had been punished enough.

Ms. Emory and the principal held a joint conference with my parents and my stepmother. I guess that they decided that I was the one who should be at school, because my mother really backed down. I continued to see more of her, but now we went on shopping trips or out to dinner together. Even my stepmother became a little less possessive and began to give me more breathing space.

Ms. Emory explained to me that during a painful divorce

or separation, parents don't always do what's in their own best interest or what's right for their child. It's a difficult time for everyone, and sometimes judgment becomes clouded by emotions. She asked me to try to be understanding and to forgive my parents. I do forgive them, but I'm still glad that Ms. Emory was there to set things right. It's hard enough to go to school and get good grades without outside interference from your family.

DIEM

"They don't really want us as their close friends"

I came to America with my family from Vietnam. We were fortunate to be able to leave when we did. In Vietnam my father had been a physician who was known as being sympathetic to American involvement there.

If we'd been denied entry to the United States, my whole family might have been killed when the communists took over. I know that thousands of people like us were murdered for their associations with Americans, and even less. But still, it's difficult to leave the country where you were born and grew up. You leave behind all your friends and memories. But most of all you leave a place where you belonged.

There's so much that is wonderful about America. Finally, we feel safe. Everyone in my family is working hard to build a new life. I feel lucky to have survived—I know that many young Vietnamese people did not. Still, after attending high school in the United States, I wonder if I'll ever feel that I really belong again.

New Asian immigrants face some prejudice just about everywhere they go. I had heard about racism in America, but I thought that it was mostly between blacks and whites or between whites and Spanish-speaking people. But there have been instances when all three of these groups have turned on us.

I know that living in America has been hard for some of the black and other minority group kids. It must be miserable to have been born right here and still sometimes be treated as though you were an outsider or a second-rate person.

Some of the black kids at my school are already discouraged. They think that if they're never going to be able to get a good job, why should they bother studying now. Kids younger than me who speak fluent English have given up on their futures because of their skin color.

At best, the majority of black and Hispanic kids at our school get automatically channeled into vocational education programs. If they have trouble reading, instead of being given help, they are gently encouraged to set small goals. But I can't believe that with some extra help they couldn't do better.

I only recently learned to read and write English, and now I'm getting A's in my English classes. Maybe the difference is that I haven't given up. I'm determined to do well in America and to make something of myself. But maybe it's different for very poor kids who believe that they may end up on a street corner drinking liquor from a bottle in a paper bag.

I try to understand what the others are going through, but that still doesn't make me feel any better when they call me Chink or Princess Fu Chin-Chang. I'm not even Chinese, but to them all Asians are Chinese. They don't see any differences between us. For some people at school who have nothing better to do we're just a vulnerable new group to put down. They can't see that taunting us isn't going to improve their situation. But some are very angry and do it just the same.

Some of the white kids at school are no better. They'll laugh among themselves while they imitate our speech by jabbering. It still hasn't occurred to them that the Vietnamese students can speak two languages fluently, while most of them can only speak one.

I can't understand why some of them are so mean to us for no reason at all. They don't even know us—we haven't done anything to them. In my history class we learned that at one time America was called the melting pot because it was a country made up of people from so many different places. If you go back far enough, no one except the Native Americans were here originally. At one time or another just about every American family started out as foreigners.

Some of the kids we go to school with leave us alone, but most of the time they don't really want us as their close friends. Lots of the new Asian kids have really done well in class, and at times this has earned us the tolerance or even the respect of some of our more studious classmates. But almost never are we really accepted. When you walk into the school cafeteria, you'll usually see groups of Asian kids sitting together.

DIEM

I've put as much time and energy into making American friends as I've put into my schoolwork. If I'm going to live here for the rest of my life, I want the people around me to mean something. But lately I've finally caught on to the fact that there are unsaid standards for acceptance within the overall picture.

For example, if you don't dress right, forget it. No one will be caught dead being seen with you. American young people have determined the correct shoes, jeans, shirts, and sweaters for social success. Teenagers in this country must be making American clothing manufacturers very wealthy.

I've tried hard to fit in. I've even taken a part-time job to pay for the clothes that may help to ward off rejection. I've made a few American friends now, but they still never seem to let me forget the differences between us.

A couple of weeks ago I went to the mall with two of my girlfriends. We bought some T-shirts and then headed for the department store's cosmetic counter. We were discussing what color eye shadow and liner to buy, when one of the girls suggested that I only get lipstick and blush.

She said that eye makeup wouldn't be good for me because when I smiled my eyes disappeared anyway. She was supposed to have been my friend. I wondered how she could have been so mean. I had let her copy my math homework countless times. Couldn't she see how much a remark like that hurt? Similar incidents have often happened. I sometimes wonder if all the trouble I've gone to in order to make friends at school has been worth it.

I later went back to the mall to buy the eye makeup. It might be useful to me after all, because sometimes when I'm at school I don't feel like smiling very much.

EDDIE

"That school offered me
a new life"

NO one in my family ever finished high school, and until about a year and a half ago, it looked like I was going to carry on the family tradition. I hated school and I tried to stay as far away from it as I could. I'd much rather have been hanging out with my older brother and his friends.

To me, school was just a place where dumb teachers tried to force you into a straitjacket. I'd rather be dead than let that happen to me. But hanging out with my brother wasn't always so great either. He and his friends were always getting into trouble—a couple of them were even sent to a juvenile detention center upstate.

Sometimes, even if I'd cut school to be with them, my brother or his friends would decide that I was too young to come along. When this happened I wasn't able to go back home until four o'clock because then my mother would know that I hadn't gone to school. So a lot of the time avoiding school meant a long, boring day. But often I stayed out anyway because I figured that it couldn't be more boring outside than inside.

Where I lived there weren't many places around to go to. And unfortunately the school district's truancy officer was alert to what few there were. He made the rounds during school hours in his county car, picking up kids like me and bringing us back. After I got in trouble with the law a couple of times, a juvenile court judge gave me a choice—I could either regularly attend this new special school as well as see a court-appointed counselor, or spend time in a special residence for boys.

And that's how I decided that school was where I wanted to be. I remember thinking that I'd have to do time in the lesser of two jails. But after only a few hours at my new school, I realized just how wrong I was.

I was enrolled in one of those experimental alternative schools in the city. The classes were held in an old, dilapidated school building, but after stepping through the door, it became clear that you were not in an ordinary school.

For one thing, the classrooms looked different. Some had couches and lounge chairs arranged as they might be in a living room. The instructors sat alongside the kids rather than at a separate desk at the room's front. Our classes were small, and there were always at least two teachers present. Sometimes we worked as a group, sometimes alone, but at this school everyone was treated equally.

Each student was assigned a counselor to see individually. The counselors and teachers were more like friends than disciplinarians, and if there was an area you were having difficulty with, you were assigned a private tutor from among the student-teachers at school.

The actual courses were also interesting. We studied poetry by examining rock music lyrics. Students having difficulty with writing or math could improve their skills by using a series of computer games. Some of the programs were like video arcade games. I must have fed thousands of quarters to those machines in the past when I had nothing to do all day.

Although the kids at my school didn't have the greatest history in terms of getting along, most of us were okay here. There was no need to break the rules. All of us voted on our own restrictions. Anyone who caused trouble had to answer to the rest of the students, and some of these kids were tougher than the teachers at regular school.

The feeling you got about what was happening was great. We all wanted our school to work. And for the first time many of us now looked forward to a goal we thought we'd never achieve—becoming high school graduates. The former failures had become successful in school. We were doing okay. And we weren't going to let anyone take that from us.

In addition to our regular class periods, there were also special trips and projects. Some kids studied earth science by going on camping trips upstate. The chemistry class spent a week at a pharmaceutical lab alongside the lab technicians. A well-known Hungarian chef taught the cooking class how to make pastries, which they shared with the rest of us during lunch period.

I chose a class in which a small group of students worked with an independent filmmaker from Los Angeles. We decided to put together a documentary film on the housing crisis in America. We worked hard to develop the skills necessary to produce good questions and interviewing techniques. We also had to become expert at using a video camera and developing and editing film.

But it was all worth it because the results were outstanding. Our film was so moving and well targeted that it was later shown by the mayor at a town hall meeting. And there's new talk about developing a task force to tackle the housing problem. After doing this film, that's a project I'd like to work on.

Three local newspapers did stories on the four students at our school involved in producing the film. It was wonderful to be interviewed by an actual reporter and to see my picture in the newspapers. A couple of years ago I'd have expected that my picture might instead be on a WANTED poster in the post office. That school did much more than offer me an education. It offered me a new life.

PETER

"He tries to make me into a miniature of himself"

MORE than anything else, my parents want me to be a success. The problem is that their idea of success isn't mine and hasn't been for a long time. They want a real prime time kid. If they could have things their way, I'd be an Ivy League college bound student council president. They wouldn't mind a son who was an all-around athlete and the heart throb of every blond cheerleader.

Unfortunately, or perhaps fortunately, I'm none of the above, and have never wanted to be. All that stuff is my parents' dream; it has nothing to do with me. They think of a son as a badge of their own success. But I'm a separate person, not a human barometer of my mother's or father's ability as a parent.

I've really been into music since I was about twelve. I'm a drummer and I've been with a couple of bands, but the groups never lasted for very long. Grades, competition, and getting into a good college don't mean very much to me. I know that many private colleges are really hurting for students right now, and if I can't get a music job, I'm sure that I'll get into a school somewhere. Then I'd try getting night jobs in clubs, and if the school had a decent music department, maybe I'd major in that. I'd go anywhere, just as long as it was away from home and I could concentrate on my music. It would be great to get away from school and my parents' intensity.

My parents spend a lot of time at school. It probably has to do with the fact that I cut class quite a bit and they're always being called in. Some weeks I think they're at school more than I am.

There's nothing worse than having my parents show up at school. My dad goes into his big macho act and blames everything on the teachers. Even when I tell him that right now my head isn't into going to class, he says that I don't know what I'm talking about and that if the school were doing a good job, I'd willingly attend. He's dead wrong. But my father's never listened to me in the past, so why should he start now? My dad stands up for God, country, and his son, regardless of what the circumstances are.

He finds an excuse for everything I do. Then he tries to make me into a miniature of himself. It always has to be his values, his dreams, and his ideas on how a student should deal with school.

I'm not a person to my father. He's the instructor, and I'm just a piece of chalk he uses to write his instructions on the blackboard. He treats our deans, teachers, and guidance counselors with as little respect. After he's been to my school, I dread going back there even more. It's as if I'm General Patton's son and he's declared the school his battlefield.

MICHAEL

"Nobody wants to cheat"

'VE cheated in school when I thought that I could get away with it. I'm not proud of it and I don't usually feel very good about myself afterward, but sometimes it's the only way possible to survive in a pressure cooker. My parents are really set on my getting good grades. They study my report card the same way they scrutinize the newspaper's stock market page. And they make me feel that I've got to live up to their expectations.

I can't remember my mother or father ever asking me

about what I actually learned in school or if I enjoyed a particular subject. Instead, it's always been, "How are you doing in geometry?" or "How'd your English teacher like your paper?"

It's hard to disappoint them. When my grades even begin to drop at all, I feel as though I've failed. It's an awful feeling.

Some teachers are really rough. They'll give tests containing at least one or two questions on materials we've never even covered in class. It's not always possible to come out ahead.

I don't think that most teachers understand how much we're expected to produce. Or even what good grades and our class rank can mean to us. If you want to get into a really good college, you've got to have a top academic record. Without that, all the extracurricular activities you may have engaged in can mean nothing.

But often it's like each teacher acts as if his is the only subject we have. They think nothing of piling on our homework or giving surprise quizzes. Sometimes we have to take two or three tests in different subjects on the same day. I'd like to see a lot of adults I know preparing for that.

When the work load becomes too difficult, some kids may resort to cheating. If you have three or four subjects to study for, you're not going to be able to devote enough time to each subject in order to be well prepared for each class.

Nevertheless, you're still expected to ace everything. And you'll usually end up cheating in the classes you are least prepared for. Those usually turn out to be the subjects you don't like or tend to do poorly in. It may be the only way left to live up to your parents' expectations and compete with the top students in the class.

MICHAEL

Everybody knows that if you cheat, it's crucial not to get caught. Few things can cause more of an uproar. Once my older brother got caught cheating on a math final. My parents acted as though he'd committed a federal offense. The assistant principal called them to school, but although the incident sparked several conferences, I don't think that anybody ever really understood what my brother was going through. We're just supposed to perform exceptionally as well as always act honestly, but how many adults can actually live up to the standards they set for us?

My father has gotten countless traffic tickets for parking in no-parking zones or for not coming to a full stop at stop signs. And you're always hearing about people who don't file their income tax honestly. Sometimes they're even admired for their cunning in cheating the IRS. How about all the corruption in government? Successful adults often accept dishonesty in order to achieve their business goals. Are kids the only ones who are supposed to be perfect?

Most of my friends have cheated on tests in school at one time or another. The kids who never cheat are usually either afraid of getting caught or just don't know how to do it safely. Nobody wants to cheat. But if it's a choice of being honest or of getting a grade, most kids will try for the A. That may sound wrong, but we didn't make the rules, we're just trying to get by.

TOM

"Several menacing gangs"

"OKAY, give up the jacket," Ace muttered, clasping his large hand around my throat as he pushed my body straight against the steel metal lockers behind us. It was clear that I was not going to get out of this one easily. In what seemed like less than an instant, I had been surrounded by members of Ace's gang. They were all bigger than me, and they closed in around me to form a semicircle in front of the lockers. I felt nearly crushed—I could scarcely breathe. But they moved in tightly so that I was completely hidden from passersby in the hall. Not that anybody would have stopped anyway. Everybody looked out for himself at our school. You went to class at your own risk.

That day there was no point in resisting Ace's demands. It was clear that he and his friends were going to get the jacket one way or another. I knew that these guys were armed with more than muscles. Ace carried a blade. Flip and Tyron had screwdrivers that they had sharpened to a fine point. The guys at our school, especially those who were in gangs, equipped themselves with an assortment of armaments. I was among the small minority who carried only pencils, notebooks, and books to class.

Ace unbuttoned my jacket. Following his lead, two of the other guys slid the coat from my shoulders and down my arms. In order to get their prize, they knocked the books I had tightly clutched from my hands. I think that the humiliation of what had happened to me was even worse than losing the jacket. There was nothing I could do about it. I only hoped that they couldn't feel me shake as they went through their maneuvers.

By now they were certain that the jacket was theirs, given up easily to them without any trouble from me. They were taking it slowly to savor the enjoyment of exercising their power. They knew that they were in charge at school and they liked it that way.

The kids like me, who mainly came to school to graduate, weren't going to be a problem to them. As far as they were concerned, we had our place at school too. To them, we were walking stores—open during school hours as well as shortly before and after the morning and dismissal bells sounded. The clothes on our backs, our jewelry and money, the candy and food we bought or brought were considered available merchandise.

Sometimes I felt like a walking display unit for a department store. The newer, more valuable your things were, the more vulnerable you became. I wasn't the only kid who felt that way. It was an unsaid fact. Our school had been taken over by several menacing gangs who sort of hung out together in a loose alliance in order to divide up the turf.

Everybody was scared of them. They had battled the staff for years and had obviously won. We had had a new principal every year. Each one would begin the term acknowledging the terrible conditions at school and proclaiming how he or she was going to change things. We had had all types and each had a unique or experimental strategy for turning things around.

There were the strict disciplinarians who would have been better off in the military, as well as the ones who tried to befriend the misunderstood bullies. In the end the only thing that they had in common was their defeat. None of them lasted past their first year. Some of them didn't even make it through the first term.

All our principals have been victims of gang pranks. Sometimes it was harmless stuff like letting the air out of their car tires. Usually they'd try this stunt on a daily basis in order to wear the person down.

If they couldn't break the guy right off, they'd go further. Few principals left our school without having had the filthiest graffiti imaginable sprayed all over both their cars and homes. More severe measures might be used against a principal considered to be resistant.

One of our principals had his seven-year-old son kidnapped. A group of them grabbed the little kid from off the street while the child was walking home from school alone. They dragged him into their car, blindfolded him, and then took him to an abandoned apartment to terrorize him. They kept waving blades in front of the kid's face. They also took turns holding him up to a hanging noose they had hooked up from the ceiling. They threatened to kill both him and his mother if his father, our principal, didn't leave them alone.

After a few hours they put the kid back in the car and drove around for a while. Then they pushed the boy out of the car about two blocks from his home. He was still blindfolded at the time. As it turned out, the child was unable to identify the boys who had taken him. He seemed too confused to be of any real help to the police in determining exactly where he'd been taken. The guys were never caught, but the principal resigned that June.

It was the same story with the teachers. All the decent teachers put in for transfers. Some, whose transfers weren't granted, just quit. My father used to say jokingly that our school was probably more responsible for setting teachers on the fast track to new careers than anything else in their lives.

It was obvious that the teachers who stayed on were only concerned with self-preservation. In that respect they weren't really that different from the rest of us. They hadn't actually taught kids anything in years. They struggled to survive in order to collect their paychecks and eventually their pensions.

Occasionally, somebody young, bright, and enthusiastic would come along. A teacher, usually just out of college, who was going to leave his mark on our lives. Those types usually left after the first month or two of school.

Most of our teachers were little more than police officers. They tended to stay out of the way of the tough kids and tried to enforce their discipline on us. Often, they'd turn our regular class periods into study halls. This meant that the teacher read the newspaper or a magazine while the kids did whatever they wanted. Usually within minutes of that kind of announcement, papers and candy were flying across the room and kids were jumping from desk to desk. Anybody with a radio would usually turn it on.

Some kids left the classroom to wander the halls, hang out in the girls' or boys' room, or go to the candy store to play video games. Only when the noise sounded like mob rule and things seemed really out of hand would the teacher react. Then he might look up from his newspaper to say, "Let's keep the noise down." And it wasn't unusual for a teacher to leave the room for twenty minutes or more himself.

I, along with some others like me, lived a waking nightmare. We were supposed to be in school in order to learn something and to better our lives, but usually we were made to feel more like victims. The worst part of the ghetto had invaded our school and taken it over. You didn't go to class to stay off the streets, because the building itself had become as dangerous as the worst sections of town. You couldn't help but feel fearful because the tough guys were at school—not to attend class but to stalk the grounds.

Not everybody who lives in our neighborhood joins a gang, is hooked on drugs, or holds up gas stations or candy stores. My parents try to give their kids a decent life. I want a good life, but right now I'm just concerned with living through the end of this term.

I have a part-time job at a fast food service after school and on weekends. I want to be a commercial artist, and I'm saving a lot of what I earn for my art school tuition after I graduate high school. I had also used some of the money to buy a replacement for the new jacket that Ace and his gang took. I should never have worn that jacket to school, but I guess that I couldn't resist wearing it and having other people see me in it. It felt so good to have it on.

My mother always says that if you can pay for anything with just money, you're fortunate. I guess that I'm lucky because I wasn't hurt. Some kids have been roughed up pretty bad by the gangs.

Once when they tried to rip a gold chain from a guy's neck, the chain didn't break off easily because it was pretty solid and heavy. Instead of allowing the kid to undo the clasp, they pulled the chain, dragging the young boy the full length of the gravel schoolyard. By the time the necklace finally broke off, the kid's neck and chin had been pretty torn up by the gravel. Three of his teeth had broken. And he had also fractured a rib.

I can hold my own all right in a fair fight, but that's really not what I want for myself. I hate getting up in the morning and then having to think about who I'll have to take on that day. If you live in my neighborhood and go to my school, you either fight or you're nothing.

I need to get out of here. What keeps me going is that I think that an end to all this is in sight. Hopefully, this is my last term at this school, or what I like to call the house of horrors. I guess that I'm one of the lucky ones. My artistic talent was my ticket out. In the city there are a number of really good public schools, but admission to them is competitive and the entrance standards are high. I applied to the High School of Art and Design. It's an outstanding art school, it's free, and maybe best of all—it's civilized. I had to submit samples of my best artwork as well as undergo a series of interviews with the faculty board. Nearly two weeks later, I received my acceptance letter.

Knowing that I only have to stay here for a few more months helps to make the situation more bearable. But I really feel sorry for the decent kids who didn't have the chance that I did and are forced to remain. Even if you go to our school wanting to get an education, it's nearly impossible to learn anything anyway. In an atmosphere of violence and cruelty, it takes all your energy just to survive. To call that building a school is ridiculous.

SHERRY

"She was fashionably thin"

I weigh more than I want to and it makes me hate myself. Sometimes, I feel like the original Elephant Girl. Mrs. Lewis, our health teacher at school, is always telling me that I'm not fat. And actually, I'm really not all that fat. Certainly, the circus fat lady is way out ahead of me in excess poundage.

In reality, I'm just pudgy, unattractively so. If I were an inanimate object, I'd be a chunky chocolate bar rather than a Virginia Slims cigarette. Get the picture? Mrs. Lewis says that men like women with a little meat on their bones. But sometimes I think that although she works in a high school, perhaps Mrs. Lewis doesn't really know very many young boys.

All the popular girls at school are thin—exceptionally so. Sometimes I feel as if I hate them—even the nice ones. Other times I experience a combined sort of hate and envy toward the skinny girls. At our school it's like this—very thin girls with good wardrobes are considered good-looking. Not if they have an atrocious face, of course. But even with just fairly decent features, they are considered good-looking if their reedlike bodies are draped in the right garments.

Guys make miserable cracks about overweight girls, and the girls at school are even worse. They'll pick you apart as though you were a leftover leg of cold chicken waiting in the refrigerator to be devoured. And I'm not kidding—these girls are experts at finding flaws. If your stomach isn't perfectly flat, they'd say that you looked pregnant. Bulges and overlapping layers of fat (no matter how miniscule) are totally unacceptable.

Patti Lincroft, a ninth-grader with gorgeous blond hair and creamy pink skin (without blusher), got Nick Armstrong, one of the most popular guys on the football team, to take her out. You couldn't really call Patti fat, but most of the girls at school did anyway. She wasn't really fat, she just didn't have a string bean figure. Patti was curvy, and most of the guys went wild over the way she looked in clinging outfits.

Well, the skinnies really started in on her. I think that a lot of it came out of sheer jealousy. It was unusual for someone with the popularity and prestige of Nick Armstrong to go out with any freshman girl. And yet Patti, who didn't look like a released concentration camp victim, had accomplished just that with seemingly little effort.

But as soon as Pat and Nick were seen together at the pizza parlor, it all started. The really vicious older thinnies began calling Patti FAT PAT. They teased Nick about going out with such a cute little pudge ball. Christiana, a super-skinny senior, sarcastically assured Nick publicly that he needn't be concerned about Patti's weight problem. She said that she was certain that Fat Pat was still insulated with baby fat, which she'd probably shed in time.

That did it. Christiana's boyfriend, who was on the football team, along with some of his friends were unable to resist joining in on the fun. From then on it was Nick & Porky, as in Porky Pig. It was everywhere. Drawn in chalk cupid hearts on benches, the sidewalk, and in both the girls' and boys' bathrooms at school. Incredible as it may seem, this is what happened to an exceptionally pretty young blonde who was just a little overweight.

Nick buckled under the pressure. He stopped seeing Patti. He told her that it had nothing to do with the jokes, he just felt that he wanted to see other people. Too young to go steady—the whole bit. What a lot of garbage. Patti didn't buy it, and I don't think that anybody else did either for that matter.

Maybe his actions don't say very much for Nick. He couldn't take the ribbing. But that's just the way it is at my school. If you're not in, you're out. And right now for girls thin is in.

I felt awful about what happened to Patti. I really identified with the anguish she must have felt over being publicly humiliated that way. Before Nick Armstrong took an interest in her she was considered only as a pretty, if slightly plump, girl. Now after several innocent dates with the school's football hero, she had become known as "The Pig."

Not being a man who puts very much stock in his own judgment, shortly afterward Nick Armstrong began going with another girl. So much for seeing a lot of different people. His new choice was Sara Bichon, a skeletonlike senior. Sara did have beautiful clothes, but it was easy for her to look well dressed. Sara's family was quite well-off, and Sara was an only child. She'd been a spoiled brat ever since anyone could remember. She trots herself around dressed like Princess Di.

Looking at her face, Sara Bichon is not nearly as pretty as Patti. But she was considered more desirable than Patti nonetheless. She had fashionable clothes, and she was fashionably thin. People were impressed with the way she looked.

My parents have assured me time after time that excessive dieting in order to meet the unrealistic standards of others demonstrates a lack of concern for one's good health as well as poor judgment. But who can consider health and judgment when you want a boyfriend so badly that you're practically willing to starve yourself to get one. And if Patti's experience with a really popular boy from school proved so horrendous, what could I possibly expect? I'd been told that I was attractive, but I didn't have Patti's long, blond, flowing hair or a peaches and cream complexion.

Practically every girl I know at school is on a diet. If you let yourself get out of shape, you're considered a slob. Someone who is out of control. And that's just what most people either silently think or publicly say about you.

I remember how one Sunday a few months ago my parents took us all out to dinner to celebrate my grandmother's birthday. The food was delicious and I really binged. Somehow I just couldn't seem to stop myself. I started off with a salad, which wouldn't have been bad if I hadn't topped the greens with gobs of blue cheese dressing.

Next there was the creamy New England clam chowder, followed by a huge steak and french fries. For dessert I ordered a chocolate milk shake and blueberry pie with a scoop of cherry vanilla ice cream on top. It was wonderful, but as soon as I finished the last forkful, I began to feel guilty. I was used to it. By now it had become a familiar feeling. A feeling that nearly always followed an eating binge.

Throughout the long ride home, I felt nothing but contempt for myself and for what I had done. How could I have eaten so much and done that to my body again? Did I want to turn into an ugly version of pretty Patti—alias Porky Pig? Did I want to become one of the famous fat girls at school? Girls who were social rejects. Girls who spent their Saturday nights going out together instead of going out with boys. Would someone ever ask me if I'd considered becoming a fashion model? Not a chance if I kept up at this rate.

I couldn't stop chiding myself for devouring all those forbidden foods. In fact, I was so busy beating myself up mentally for overeating that I couldn't even pay attention to what my grandmother was saying to me. And after all, we were celebrating her birthday. That Sunday might have been my grandmother's birthday, but at that moment my only concern was of unloading the hoard of food from my stomach.

My mother had been able to control herself. All she ordered was a salad without dressing and a fish fillet broiled without butter. My mother was a housewife. She didn't even have to face the kids at school. There was already a man in her life—my father. Why couldn't I have shown the same restraint?

That night when I went to bed I tried to put the binging incident behind me. I told myself not to think about it. That I'd make up for it by eating less tomorrow.

But the next morning when I woke up I hated myself even more than before. I felt fat. Even the slacks that I tried on to wear to school seemed tighter. I wanted to die. I felt like a balloon. I wished that I could have just stuck a pin into myself to deflate my protruding stomach.

I couldn't handle the thought of going to school that day. I didn't want anyone to see me. I lied to my mother and told her that I was too sick to go. Fortunately, she believed me.

I spent the rest of the day at home hating myself and trying not to eat anything. Sometimes when I overeat, I force myself to throw up. So many of the girls at school do that. If they have an opportunity for a few minutes of privacy after their cafeteria periods, they go into a bathroom stall in the girls' room at school and gag themselves.

I've done it myself sometimes. I know that a lot of girls at school do it, although they deny it. You just have to go into the girls' room following lunch. You can hear them behind the locked doors of the toilet stalls.

Eating a lot and throwing up is called bulimia. We saw a movie on it in health education. And even though I'm certain that over 95 percent of the girls in the class must have tried it at least once, everyone acted as if a rare disease from the South Seas were being described. Everybody said it was disgusting and gross and wondered aloud how someone could do that. What hypocrites—even me. As I left that class, I couldn't help wonder whether the rush to the bathroom after lunch that day would be lessened. It wasn't.

I know that throwing up after you eat isn't good for you, but somehow the medical consequences fade when you're faced with the possibility of gaining weight. You can never be thin enough. At school, the tall, thin girls are envied. Maybe not everybody can be tall, but anyone can be thin if she's willing to do whatever it takes—starve, throw up, exercise—whatever.

Some of the girls may have thrown up too often though. A junior at our school whom I've never met, but who was supposed to have been reed thin as well as an honors student, was recently hospitalized from the effects of bulimia. She admitted that she used to stash large quantities of junk food in her locker, which she'd eat and then vomit in the girls' room.

She told her mother that many girls at school did the same thing, and before long her mother got in touch with several other mothers whose daughters were bulimic and the group of them formed a delegation to confront the principal with the problem. Since a lot of what was going on was happening at school, they wanted to involve the faculty.

It was a topic for discussion at the PTA meeting, and after that there were some changes at school. We saw the same movie on eating disorders in health class again, and later that month a doctor and nurse team addressed a school assembly on the topic. Everybody became more knowledge-able about the whole binge-purge thing, but I don't think that many, if any, of us stopped.

When you've been doing something for a while that's supposed to be dangerous and nothing happens to you, you almost start to feel as though you're immune to the possible risks. Maybe it's a false sense of security, but you think that all you're doing is staying thin.

Besides, being overweight is so awful that I think most girls would be willing to chance their health in order to be slender. I've heard a lot of girls say they'd rather die than be heavy, and although they may not really mean that, it shows how they feel.

The mothers' group that had been pressuring our principal was not easily satisfied. They continued to contact still other parents in order to gain support for their cause. As a result, teachers' aides were posted in the lavatories during class changes. As there wasn't sufficient personnel available to carry out this task, volunteer mothers took turns helping out.

With the lavatories monitored during period breaks, an unusually high number of girls began raising their hands to be excused during class. It seemed apparent that they were trying to avoid the monitors—even the most dedicated volunteer mothers seemed unwilling to spend all their time on toilet duty.

Some girls retaliated in other ways as well. Although we weren't supposed to leave the premises during school hours, now several girls left to eat lunch at the candy stores or in the diner, where they could use the public restrooms. I heard that some girls even brought plastic bags with them to school, and used them outside in the smoking areas when no one was looking. It looks like thin's going to win—no matter what it takes.

DANA

"Every so often you come across a gem"

think one of the most important factors in determining whether or not I'll like a subject is the teacher. The right teacher can make you look forward to a class, just as a bad teacher can make you dread coming to school. Unfortunately, at my school, the bad ones far outnumber the superior teachers, but every so often you come across a gem. Really good teachers are usually popular with most of the kids, and everyone's always trying to get into their classes.

To me, a good teacher is someone who likes the subject

he's teaching, as well as enjoys working with his students. That type of teacher keeps up with all the developments in his field, and makes learning interesting and fun.

The teacher I had for music last year was really terrific. He got permission to take our class on a trip to an actual recording studio. We made a record, and although it was never sold to a commercial label, it was played at two school assemblies as well as at a local dance. It may even take off yet—who knows? I learned a lot about music in that class and really had a good time.

Most kids think that it's important for a teacher to be fair. You can look up to a teacher who's fair, even if you don't get a top grade in the class. At least you know that you've earned whatever grade you received. But a lot of teachers aren't fair, and that's true even for some of the ones who think that they are.

Several of the teachers don't seem at ease with minority group kids. They try too hard. A few of the white teachers celebrate Black History Month more rigorously than our black faculty members. They continually stress black pride and so openly gush over their black students that it's obvious that they're embarrassing some of the black kids. Sonia, one of my black friends, says that she hates coming to school in February (Black History Month) because she doesn't enjoy being made the center of attention.

Other teachers are even worse. Those are the ones who seem to be totally unaware of how they come across. They have their obvious favorites in class who receive special treatment. Usually they tend to like the better-looking, well-dressed kids, but sometimes they may react to a student personally—like when a teacher is partial to a particular girl because that student resembles her daughter.

Once a teacher stops seeing his students objectively, it

becomes nearly impossible for him to remain fair and impartial in class. A teacher is supposed to use his skills to help a student learn, instead of using a young person to build up his ego. It's hard for me to respect a teacher, or anyone for that matter, who is unfair. And it's equally difficult to learn anything from a person whom you don't respect.

JERRY

"Part of the grade game"

FOR most of us, success in school has very little to do with actual learning. The most important thing you have to master is how to play the grade game. Once you devise your own strategies for getting high marks, everything opens up to you. You may be admitted to a prestigious college or win a scholarship, not to mention gaining the admiration of your teachers and parents.

It's really just a matter of putting all the puzzle pieces together in a predictable manner. It's not always the smartest or most creative kids who get the highest grades. There isn't much room for individuality or even for people who tend to look at things just a little differently. Generally, the accolades and awards are reserved for the parrots and the flatterers. The people who know how to give the teachers what they want, whether it's on a test paper or in a class discussion. The people who fit in well with the system.

When you're taking a test and you know that your grade depends on the result of that examination, any interest you might have had in the subject's content becomes secondary to trying to read the teacher's mind in attempting to supply the answer he wants. Whatever you've learned about the subject becomes of little consequence if it isn't what's been asked for on the test. The test grade to a large extent supposedly reflects your subject knowledge. It may have a tremendous bearing in how you fare in the course. And therefore it becomes more important than anything else you might have gotten out of the class.

Not everyone does well on tests. At times, it can almost turn into a ridiculous game of hit and miss. Some kids haven't mastered the art of test taking, some panic under pressure or need more time or another way to express what they know.

Often kids who are having problems at home find it hard to concentrate on taking a test. In many cases it's not that they're stupid or even that they don't know the work, but usually they're the ones left by the wayside. The ones who don't make it.

Being an academic success means learning the ins and outs of the school system. Then you have to work things to your advantage. A lot of kids are already doing it without even realizing it.

Take selecting courses for example. Before scheduling

your classes, it's essential to learn as much as you can about who's teaching what from the older kids. You have to find out who's an easy grader as well as who's really tough. Some teachers give tests taken directly from the class notes. It's important to know this because if you have to cram for another exam, you can skip reading the book in this case. Most of the teachers only require that you're good at memorizing and are able to mindlessly spit back what was said in class.

It's just about guaranteed that these teachers will give you an A if you do the work. You just rehash the class periods on your test papers. A few of the teachers require a little more thinking in your answers. Although their classes may seem more challenging and thought provoking, you can never be sure what unusual questions will turn up on their tests. If there's a chance of doing poorly in a subject they've studied for, most kids will try to avoid these teachers. The pressure on us to come out on top is so great that we can't afford to take risks.

Getting high grades also depends on becoming aware of each teacher's little idiosyncracies. For example, everyone in school knows that Mrs. Philips, who teaches ninth grade English, is crazed when it comes to neatness. At times she doesn't even seem rational about it. It's almost as if to her a tidy but poorly thought out paper is worth more than one which is on target and well written but isn't as neat.

Even if you're only an average English student, you can still get an A with Mrs. Philips if you've done a perfectly manicured typing job and then placed the finished product in one of those fancy-looking colored folders that you can buy at a stationery store or in the five and ten. That trick always works with her. Mrs. Philips will think that you spent hours on the paper and you're sure to get a really high mark on it.

JERRY

You need to learn all you can about the teachers in order to come up with a class program that will be to your personal advantage. There are some courses that everyone in an academic program has to take. Those are the required courses, and there's no way around them. You're most likely to do well if you try to pick the easiest teachers possible for the required courses. It may mean changing an elective that you wanted to take or having an inconvenient schedule, but it's a sure way to keep up your grade average.

Once I'd selected the teacher whom I'd wanted for chemistry only to find that my guidance counselor had me slated for another period. Science has always been difficult for me. With a tough teacher I'd be likely to pull a low B in the course and my class rank would probably go down. I'm among the top twenty kids now, and I need to at least break into the top ten in order to get into a big name college.

I had to take chemistry, so one day in between classes I talked to the teacher I had originally wanted. I told him how I'd heard what a really good teacher he was, and how disappointed I was that I'd have to graduate without having been in his class. I lied. It worked.

I had counted on the chemistry teacher being human, and he was. I wasn't proud of myself for what I did. But I considered it part of the grade game we're pushed into playing to even get a shot at going to the best schools.

A lot of that kind of thing goes on at school on almost every level. When you apply to most colleges, you need to supply reference letters from your teachers. The fonder they are of you, the better the picture they are likely to paint. Besides, when a teacher is not sure whether to give a student an A-minus, or a B-plus, his personal impression of the kid has somehow got to be taken into account.

There's a lot of competition at my school, even among

friends. It's almost as if we're pitted against one another in a race to win the teacher's approval. Success is so important to those at the top that just about anything can be justified in order to get it. Anyway, the chemistry teacher I had wanted simply talked to the guidance counselor, and by that afternoon I had been assigned to his class.

Planning elective or nonrequired courses is easier. If there are some tough courses that you've got to take with difficult teachers, it's important to take a couple of easy subjects to make certain that your grade average remains high. Few people can always get As in everything.

The result of all this is that the Spanish kids take Spanish and the Chinese kids take Chinese, although they already know these languages. They might profit more from learning a new language, but usually they feel forced to take the easy way out. It's all got to do with the pressure for grades. The drive to learn something new and worthwhile, or even to try something that looks interesting but that you're not quite sure you'd be able to master, has to be channeled elsewhere. Most parents seem to feel that going to school is the only thing a kid has to do, and you're expected to do it well.

When I tell this to people outside the school scene, often they'll ask me what all this has to do with learning. I have to admit—not much. In school the pressure for grades far outweighs the joy and interest you might experience in learning something new. While you're in a classroom setting, actual understanding is not as important as making the teacher think that you have a grasp of the material. I'm little more than a young runner in the junior rat race. My dad works in an advertising firm, and he's always saying that he has to give his clients what they want. He says that he has to understand their expectations in order to come up with a working formula.

Students do much of the same thing. We have to come up with the right answers. And although in real life there may be more than one acceptable solution, most teachers do not afford us that kind of leeway in class. Generally, there's only one right answer. Any other way of tackling a problem becomes, at best, less right. At school you exchange the right answers for a high grade, and at graduation you trade in your class credits for the badge or diploma. Then you try to get into the best college possible, and the whole thing starts all over. You become so interested in achieving that it's hard to examine if you've actually learned anything meaningful along the way.

Whenever a standardized test is given that reflects on the school or on the quality of teaching done there, the teachers do the same thing that the kids do. Whatever we're studying is put aside so that they have enough time to prepare us for the examination.

Most of my sophomore year English class was spent memorizing vocabulary words for the verbal segment of the SAT. We had all kinds of quizzes, both written and oral. Then we'd have to use the words in sentences until their meanings were firmly drummed into our heads.

Whole class periods were devoted to this pursuit for much of the year. For the most part, our school achieved its desired results. A good portion of our class scored highly on the verbal SAT. But what about delving into literature?

I know that the class time was spent this way in order to help us get into college. So I guess that you have to reason that we'll study literature there. That is if we're not off practicing for some exam to get into graduate school.

Still, what about the kid who planned to go to college and changes his mind. Or has to put off going on for financial reasons. That person will graduate with an English background consisting largely of reading comprehension skills and a formidable vocabulary of which he may use only a few words. It's probably better than nothing at all, but I can't help thinking that there should be more, much more, than the smattering of books we read and discuss in class.

My social studies teacher says that a democratic society needs an educated populace, but I don't think we're really learning anything important in school. Despite the often-spouted lofty rhetoric, school is really little more than a business.

Students need to digest the company rules and then play up to the bosses or faculty if they are going to succeed. The problem is that the customers or students and their parents are footing the bill for all this through their taxes or tuition payments. Unfortunately, I think that it's the only business where the customer isn't always right.

MOOSE

"My humiliation"

THEY called me Moose. Not my parents. Of course they wouldn't name their child that. The kids in my junior high stuck me with that nickname. They did it because they thought of me as being large, tall, and awkward—overly so.

It made me miserable. Although some king-sized guys might not mind being referred to as Moose, it was difficult for me. I wasn't the captain of the football team. I was a girl. I hated that name and I hated the kids who gave it to me. They were the same kids who wouldn't stop, who refused to let up and allow me to have a peaceful day even once in a while.

Taunting me and turning me into a cartoon character somehow made them feel superior. Calling me Moose made them feel that they were better than me. I paid for their fun with my humiliation.

How do you handle being called Moose? At first I cried. But that just gave them too much pleasure. In fact, it seemed to worsen the problem. Once I had to walk past a group of really popular kids at school. All I did was walk by, but that alone gave them enough ammunition. I had turned myself into a moving target.

Usually, I'd do just about anything to avoid walking past a group like that. If I had the chance, I'd quickly turn the other way, go down an extra flight of stairs, even walk into the wrong classroom and walk right out again before anybody had had a chance to notice that I'd actually been there.

But this time there was no way out for me. I had to either walk past them or plunge straight into the principal's office. I hadn't gone more than three feet when they began to give out loud moose calls. They became so noisy that Mr. Martin, our English teacher, had to come out of his room to break it up. But by that time they already had everyone in the hall laughing hysterically.

I remember that at the time I wished I'd never been born. I ran to the girls' room. Fortunately, one of the toilets was vacant. I sat down on the seat and cried. I wouldn't come out until all the other girls had left the room. Everyone's hair had been brushed, all the pots of lip gloss exchanged and applied, and the polished bouncing beauties had trotted off to class. The bustling room had suddenly become still. Outside, the halls had finally settled down. They seemed almost silent.

Nearly twenty minutes had passed. And as I realized that the next period was already underway, I found myself faced with a dismal prospect. I had to walk into Mr. Martin's English class without a pass for being late. Was I supposed to tell my favorite English teacher in front of the whole class that I was late because I'd just finished a long cry in the toilet?

Mr. Martin was a kind, sympathetic, and wonderfully delicious-looking man. I had always looked forward to his class. Besides, English was my best subject. He'd probably understand, but of course I wouldn't tell him anyway. I think I'd rather die. I thought about cutting the class completely. I could hide in the toilet for the rest of the period. But I thought that not showing up might really annoy Mr. Martin, and I'd still have no explanation for my absence.

I decided to brave it and attempt going to class. I'd tell Mr. Martin that I had become ill and had gone to the girls' room rather than to the nurse's office. That would explain why I was minus the pass. If I was stopped in the hall by a teacher for not having a pass en route to Mr. Martin's class, I'd tell the same story. If I made it to class and Mr. Martin sent me to the vice principal's office for not having a pass, I'd repeat the same story there.

If there was any justice in the world, Mr. Martin would be his sweet self and not get me into trouble. My seat was near the door. I could quickly slide into it without having to walk across the room. If everything went well, it would be an easy entrance.

I did it. Things couldn't have gone better. As I timidly stood in the classroom's doorway, Mr. Martin smiled broadly at me and gently said, "Hi, Lynn. C'mon in and take your seat." That was all. I couldn't believe it. No questions asked. I wouldn't have to account for the lapsed time. I'd been spared the humiliation. But of course, I realized soon enough that it had been Mr. Martin who had broken up their fun to begin with.

As I lowered myself onto my seat, a feeling of relief swept over my body. And then it started. The sound came up slowly from the back of the room to pierce my ears. It was accompanied by barely muffled laughter. I recognized what had now become a familiar noise. I had just heard a long, low moose call.

Once again it was Mr. Martin to the rescue. He stopped the class to tell Joshua—the tall, handsome, iron-hearted boy whose turn it had been that day to ruin my life—that he'd see him at detention that afternoon. Mr. Martin added that Joshua could make all the noises he wished while he remained after school, but asked Josh to spare us his infantile act for the duration of the period.

The rest of the class went along smoothly enough. I tried to put everything that had happened behind me in order to concentrate on Mr. Martin's discussion of Shakespeare's *Julius Caesar*. As the bell rang, signaling the period's end, Mr. Martin asked me to remain behind for a moment to speak to him.

At that point I thought that it was all over for me. It looked as though this wasn't going to end easily after all. I was going to have to account for my whereabouts earlier this period. But Mr. Martin only said to me, "Lynn, I just wanted to tell you how pretty you look today. Your dress is beautiful. Tall women look so wonderful in the right outfits. You remind me a lot of my wife. She's as tall and lovely as yourself."

I couldn't believe it. Mr. Martin had caught me off guard.

I was barely able to speak. I felt as though my voice were trapped somewhere deep inside of me. As a hot blush crept up on my cheeks, I muttered a weak, "Thank you." Then I practically flew off to my next class.

I couldn't stop thinking about how great it would be to someday marry someone just like Mr. Martin. And it was exciting to think that Mr. Martin had married someone that I reminded him of.

My mother always says that all good things must come to an end. For me, it just happened too soon. When I arrived at my locker at the end of the day, that group of cruel kids were waiting there for me behind a corner. It was clearly an ambush. They were Joshua's friends. Did they blame me for his having to stay after school? Had I forced Josh to publicly humiliate me or something?

Anyway, apparently they had seen me crying earlier that afternoon, and they weren't about to let me get away with it. One of the girls said loudly to the group, "Hey, did you know that a Moose can cry?" "I didn't until today," another responded. Then she turned to me and said, "Tell me Lynn, can a chicken swim?" They all started laughing. I felt trapped.

And it was starting to happen again. The tears were welling up in my eyes. If I didn't escape quickly, they'd see me cry again. I bit my lip and, determined to win this time, turned from them and walked quickly toward the exit. Still, the echo of their laughter rang in my head all the way home.

I didn't go to school the next day. I told my parents that I was sick, but actually I just needed some time off to rest. I couldn't face those kids again so soon.

Later in the day I told my mother the truth about what they had said. As always, my mother tried her best to be reassuring. She explained to me for about the hundredth time how being tall was an advantage. My mother stressed that all the beauty queens and models were tall. But no matter how many times she tried to convince me, I never believed her. I was taller than nearly everyone at school, including the boys. And it only made me feel big and ugly.

I returned to school the following day. There was only about two months left until graduation. Then junior high would be over, and in the fall I'd be going to a new, large high school. I'd have to take a bus to get there, and there'd be a whole bunch of new kids to meet. In the meantime, the people at my school started to ease up a bit on me. I thought that they must have gotten bored torturing me and had sought out a new victim.

But it wasn't over. The following September, as I entered the cafeteria on my first day at the new school, a cry hit the air. At first I wasn't sure what I'd heard. There were so many kids there and the room seemed to vibrate with noise and movement. But after the second or third repeat I recognized the sound that had haunted me all of last year. It was a moose call.

Author's Note: At the time of this writing Lynn's moose-call days had ended. In her sophomore year of high school, she was selected by a panel of judges from the local chamber of commerce to represent her school modeling junior fashions at a series of county-wide fashion shows.

Lynn is currently dating a freshman from a nearby college, whom, she was quick to add, is taller than she. When asked what she remembered most fondly about junior high school, she answered, "Mr. Martin, because he took the time to make me feel worthwhile."

About the Author

Elaine Landau received her BA degree from New York University and her Masters degree in Library and Information Science from Pratt Institute.

She has worked as a newspaper reporter, an editor, and a youth services librarian, but believes that many of her most fascinating as well as rewarding hours have been spent researching and writing books and articles on contemporary issues for young people.

Ms. Landau makes her home in New York City.